THE

OF THE

HUMAN RACE

M.C. MACDONALD

Copyright M C MacDonald 2016

This book is dedicated to everything that lives on this planet.

CONTENTS

ACKNOWLEDGEMENTS iv
INTRODUCTION vi
INFANT EARTH 1
HUMANS 14
CIVILIZATION 36
MORE CIVILIZATION 87
THE INDUSTRIAL REVOLUTION 144
PRESENT DAY 191
DENIABLE REALITY 234
THE FINAL CHAPTER 248
REFERENCES 261

ACKNOWLEDGEMENTS

This book expresses the opinions of the author, and any person or group of people mentioned may or may not agree with its contents. It is intended for a general audience and references have not been cited in the text.

At this point I would like to mention that the source material for this book did not come merely from reading other books. Over the last thirty (plus) years, I have gained as much or more information from personal observation as I have from books. This is not implying that books are less important—otherwise I would not be writing one—but because books primarily acknowledge other books, I felt it necessary to mention other media.

Many hours were spend watching historical documentaries, nature programs, and many inches of file film footage on war, in an attempt to understand human behavior and life. For me, watching the real thing was as important as reading history books. I would like to extend a tremendous amount of gratitude to all the people who put together hundreds of television documentaries and nature programs.

I would also like to thank all of the archeologists, paleontologists and especially historians who have spent many years collecting and recording huge volumes of information, and meticulously ensuring the accuracy of places, dates, people, and occurrences. I would particularly like to thank Frank Sulloway for his in-depth research of Charles Darwin, which allowed me to fill in some blanks.

Over the last thirty years, I have met, associated and worked with many people, all of whom contributed in some way, although neither of us knew how at the time, so I would like to thank any person that I have crossed paths with to get to this point.

Finally, I would like to thank the staff at the local Library for putting up with me; Kathy for all her typing, editing, and enthusiasm; and Anne, whose literary skills were greatly appreciated.

INTRODUCTION

Most of what you are about to read was put down on paper in 1997, with some revisions in 1999. Some minor revisions were added quite recently (2006).

I'm sorry to say that the human race is not as intelligent as we like to think. In our extremely shortsighted, arrogant way we humans like to define ourselves as having varying degrees of intelligence, far exceeding any other creatures. I'm afraid this is not the case. On the evolutionary scale, we are not as far ahead of the other primates or mammals as we think, in fact, the difference is barely measurable. The main difference between us and the other mammals is not our intelligence, but our physical differences. Many species of mammals are probably ahead of us from an evolutionary standpoint but, because we look so much different and because we can kill anything that moves, we mistakenly believe we are somehow superior. We cannot even define intelligence and we know very little about how the brain works. Ironic, since that is how we assess intelligence.

Any books that I have read about the human race appear to be written in essentially the same way: the author studied existing historical information, or tried to define the human race based solely on one specific facet or aspect of our society (for example, archeology). The result would inevitably be a book, which describes humans as being highly intelligent throughout our history of about 5 million years or so. If we think of ourselves as being highly intelligent now, then the tendency is to push that envelope back as far as possible, partly to massage our egos, but mainly because humans are *still* not able to define intelligence. Combine that with a total ignorance about most of the other species that inhabit the planet and you have cave men being elevated to super humans. This just is not so.

This book was written from a somewhat different angle. I started some 30 years ago, to observe and to try and understand modern human behavior, and then worked *back* through history with the help of the theory of evolution. The result was an entirely different perspective of the human race. We are *not* highly intelligent now, nor have we *ever been*.

Both before and after the introduction of the theory of evolution, philosophers, biologists, archeologists, historians, paleontologists, anthropologists, scientists and other thinkers have pondered the human race, the other life forms and meaning of life. Most of these people work away in their respective fields for years but, because of their narrow focus, never seem to get any closer to understanding life, as we know it. Each of these helps significantly, but each also fails to see the *big picture*.

In order to understand life, we must combine or incorporate all of these facets of endeavor, and so throughout this book I may use one of these facets or combine two, several, or all to make some sense of the species we call human. In order to do that I felt it necessary to start at the very beginning with the creation of the universe and follow human progression right up to where we are today in order to get a more complete picture. Over the last approx. 3500 years, civilizations have gone through a series of ups and downs that we refer to as the rise, peak and decline of each civilization. Our current civilization (western democracies) is experiencing similar dynamics. If one is aware of this and accepts this historical phenomenon, then the trick is to figure out the status of our current situation and where we are in the rise, peak, decline dynamic, and if you don't want to know stop reading now.

I would like to remind readers that this is not a history book. I have not attempted to reconstruct every detail of history. Many books go into very great detail documenting places, dates, the movements of various peoples and describing interesting artifacts that have been uncovered. Historians, archeologists, and paleontologists have spent many painstaking years collecting, organizing, and dating this mountain of material, and I have no doubt that their records are complete and reasonably accurate; without such information this book could not have been written.

However, *how* we view the human race, our accomplishments, and our past history has been badly misinterpreted and considerably biased. We tend to paint quite an extraordinary picture of ourselves, despite all of the incredibly brutal, barbaric and arrogant behavior that permeates our history. And so, what I am attempting to do here is to put all of the afore mentioned information together in one book, perhaps for the first time, in a logical, cohesive explanation of life as it evolved on this planet.

I am hopeful that this book will provide a previously unknown perspective and perhaps be the beginning of a new enlightenment.

INFANT EARTH

For thousands of years humans have wondered how the universe was created. Although technology is now beginning to answer some of the many, many questions, I believe that we are still a long way from fully understanding the universe. We started by calling everything we see, the observable universe (everything that is observable by the naked eye, large telescopes, and more recently, radio waves). Interestingly enough, after many years of working on the problems, we've come up with two possible solutions: one that the universe has always existed, and the other one that it has not always existed. Many scientists have worked on this problem, including such notables as Carl Sagan; most of what you're about to read about space and creation in this chapter is based on their work.

The first theory is based on what they've referred to as the Cosmological Principle. If the universe is constant throughout time, it cannot be evolving, and must have been pretty much as it is now, and it will always be much the same. If the universe was never any different than it is today, then there was no "big bang", and no such unique event could have happened. The universe never began and never will end.

On the other hand is the "big bang" theory, which came about over the course of many, many years of various scientists proving and disproving one another's theories. The model, which seemed most likely, starts with the universe at some time as one gigantic ball; once this ball was disturbed by some force, the universe ball became unstable, exploded, and continued to expand. After billions of years of splitting apart, stars and galaxies were formed, and apparently the universe is still expanding.

Astronomers have said that measurements of light from distant galaxies show that they are receding from us and from one another, and that they are flying apart. The more remote galaxies appear to be flying apart faster than the closer galaxies. So scientists came to the conclusion that the whole universe is expanding.

At some point in the past all the material in the universe was compressed into a huge ball. Gravity in this gigantic ball would have been so intense that it would have overwhelmed all the other forces and the normal structure of matter would have been broken down.

The big bang theory does not tell us how this big ball of universal matter came into existence originally, or how long it lasted, or what made it explode. Many questions remain unanswered.

Based on earlier theories, scientists estimated that the universe was approximately 1.8 billion years old. They've now revised that to 10 to 20 billion years old, and that the earth itself is about 4.6 billion years old.

It's quite possible that some of the closest stars are hundreds of millions of light years away. The light we see tonight left the surface of those stars hundreds of millions of years ago, which means that we're seeing those stars just as they looked that long ago. This all becomes somewhat confusing, at least to me, as scientists try to unravel all of this data that they've collected, but it makes for some interesting television and big screen movies.

The big bang theory says that the universe is evolving and that if we look back in time we will see a different sort of universe. The only problem is that the distances involved are tremendous. According to the big bang model we would have to go back nearly to the beginning or at least to around 10 billion years ago in order to see any observable difference. The strongest optical telescopes cannot see much farther than 1 or 2 billion years, and once we approach a certain point we no longer have an accurate measurement of how far away the objects are.

During World War II it was discovered that if radio waves were sent out, they would bounce back from an object that they came into contact with and return back to their point of origin. By timing the interval between transmission and return, the distance to the object could be measured.

The next step was to use this radio technology in astronomy, because radio waves could be sent and received at much greater distances than the range of optical telescopes. The radio telescope can "see" 8 or 9 billion years out into the universe, compared to about 2 billion years with an optical telescope. However, these experiments did not provide any information on how the universe was created, what it was like before the explosion, or what might have caused the explosion. To this point all we have seen is a lot of other stars and galaxies.

The big bang theory says that the universe originally exploded and the fragments will keep on flying away from each other forever until each piece cools and dies. As each galaxy is receding into the distance, scientists say it is possible that it would then become attracted by the gravity of all of the other galaxies, and would be pulled back by the force of each galaxy's gravity.

This cooling process, combined with the gravitational pull, slows down the expansion and could eventually stop it. Then all of the galaxies would start to fall back toward one another, much like a large rubber band being stretched and then released. If the rubbery force of gravity is the stronger force the expansion will ultimately halt and the whole thing will snap together again.

If the whole universe comes crashing together in one place it will produce a tremendous collision. Some people are theorizing that this is what the big bang really is— an explosion resulting from the collapse of a previous universe. According to this theory the universe explodes in a big bang, expands for 10 or 20 billion years, slows down and collapses again because of its own gravity. All the galaxies rush together and collide, then explode again, creating another big bang and the whole process repeats over and over.

To prove this theory, what needs to be done is to measure the total mass of the expanding galaxies to see if it's enough to provide the necessary gravity. However, this hasn't been accomplished yet.

One of the most recent theories is that the universe began neither with a big bang nor as a steady state: it might be an accident. Many theorists feel that the universe cannot be equally balanced unless it contains equal parts of matter and anti-matter. When scientists create anti-matter in the laboratory, as soon as it touches a normal electron the two will annihilate each other, and disappear in a flash of energy. Theorists think some kind of spontaneous temporary emergence from a vacuum or white hole, comes into contact with anti-matter, and disappears.

After all is said and done, my opinion is that humans still have no real idea how the universe was created or if in fact it was created or if it has always existed. The more we study the universe the more we realize the incredible insignificance of one little planet with all of its creatures. When we consider the vastness of the universe, it's incredibly humbling. In the year 2006 scientists and astronomers claim to be making new discoveries that will tell us the origins of the universe and so we'll just have to wait and see if the aforementioned theories become obsolete.

Albert Einstein came upon something else that can't be explained: exactly what light is and how it travels. Many astronomers and scientists have used his findings and knowledge in an attempt to explain the basic fundamentals of time and space and how they relate to us on Earth.

To give you an idea of how large the universe might be, there are an estimated billion trillion stars. Based on our present technology with the *Voyager* spacecraft, it would take about 40,000 years just to reach the nearest star. Even if we did possess the technology for continuous, manned, self-sustaining space travel—there is nowhere to go.

As you're reading this, scientists are, and have been for several years, trying to design a spacecraft to travel beyond our solar system. The United States of America was seriously considering building a space ship in a program called Orion, after the constellation, and it was under development in the U.S. until the signing of the international treaty that forbids the detention of nuclear weapons in space. This space ship, which would have been built in space, would have utilized the explosion of hydrogen bombs or nuclear weapons against some type of inertial plate; each explosion would propel the craft through space.

This hypothetical space ship could conceivably travel an estimated ten per cent of the speed of light, so a trip to Alpha Centauri, one of the stars closest to Earth, would take about 43 years. These ships could possibly be used as multigenerational habitats; the people on board arriving at another star would be the descendants of those who set out some centuries before. Or, by some safe means of hibernation for humans or of cryogenic technology, space travelers could be reawakened some centuries later. I wonder how many nuclear blasts it would take to get it right.

The earth condensed out of interstellar gas and dust some 4.6 billion years ago; from studying recently discovered fossils, we now think that the origin of life happened soon afterward, around 4 billion years ago, in the ponds and oceans of what was a very young Earth.

Two theories attempt to explain how life began. One suggests that the first living things were incredibly simple one-celled organisms resulting from the necessary components, building blocks and elements all coming together in just the right combination to create a life form.

It is thought that lightning and ultraviolet light from the sun were breaking apart the simple, hydrogen-rich molecules of what was then a very primitive atmosphere and the fragments spontaneously recombined to produce more and more complex molecules.

The products of this early chemical mixture were dissolved in the oceans forming an organic concoction of gradually increasing complexity until one day a molecule arose that was able to make copies of itself using as building blocks other molecules in this primitive organic mixture. This was the earliest ancestor of what is now known as DNA.

By 3 billion years ago a number of one-celled plants joined together and the multi-cellular organisms had evolved. It appears that some form of sexual reproduction developed around two billion years ago. As more and more simple plants multiplied they produced more and more oxygen, slowly altering the original hydrogen make up. With the development of sex, two organisms could exchange their DNA code producing new varieties ready for the process of natural selection. By one billion years ago plants changed the entire environment of the earth. Green plants generated oxygen and since the oceans were then filled with simple green plants, oxygen was becoming a major constituent of the earth's atmosphere. A few primitive organisms, like botulism and tetanus bacilli, managed to survive and still exist today, even in an oxygen-free environment.

Most of the dominant forms of life for the first 4 billion years were microscopic blue-green algae, which covered and filled the oceans. By 500 million years ago there were small primitive creatures known as trilobites. The first fish and first invertebrates appeared, plants previously restricted to oceans began to colonize the land, the first insects evolved, winged insects arose, the amphibians arrived, lung fish able to survive both on land and water appeared, then the first reptiles; the dinosaurs evolved, the mammals emerged, along with the first birds, the first flowers, the earliest ancestors of the whale and dolphin and also the primates (earliest ancestors of monkeys, apes and humans).

Another theory, which is very recent, proposes that life in a very primitive form may have come to earth on comets or other meteorites traveling through space that crashed on the earth.

However, the first model seems to best suit the theory of evolution, and because scientists have been unable to find any forms of life (in space) to this point, it seems likely that this second model is not as feasible.

These theories fly in the face of creationism, which has prevailed throughout history until just recently. Creationists believe that God created the earth and all of its creatures and that there is a definite starting point for man, and that there is also a definite end point. This belief is still prevalent today although historical and archeological evidence has greatly undermined much of this way of thinking to the point where the theory of evolution is undeniable.

That's not to say that both cannot be feasible, and this book is not about denouncing creationists. Prior to the evolutionary theory, creationists believed that the earth was born between 4,500 and 6,000 years ago, depending on whom you listen to.

Many are now reluctantly accepting the evolutionary theory although forced to push back the date when they believe God created the earth. For these people, the debate now is not so much *when* it was created, but *who* the creator was.

Such a debate is not the purpose of this book. What this book hopes to accomplish is to explain what happened *after* life was created and how we got to where we are now.

* * *

We're going to back up just a little. We have very little hard evidence for the period between early simple plants and the rise of the dinosaurs. It's not until we get to the dinosaurs that we have been able to piece things together, mainly in the last 100 years. The dinosaurs provide us with some major clues as to human existence, and there is now enough evidence to fully support the theory of Evolution.

It is thought that dinosaurs arose about 230 million years ago and ruled the earth until their extinction about 65 million years ago. A few years here or there doesn't matter; the fact remains that they did rule, for about 150 million years. The dinosaurs walked the earth for a very long time and humans weren't even in the picture until millions of years later.

As the planet evolved, the landmasses and oceans moved about continuously, allowing the various species to move across large expanses of land joined by land bridges, which appeared and disappeared as the earth evolved. The climate changed, and in response to that, the plants changed and as the dinosaurs evolved, they became very specialized, and very specific about what they ate.

The dinosaurs represent one of the peculiarities of evolution. The dinosaurs thrived because of the climatic conditions and the types of plants available. There were many other species as well as the dinosaurs, including fishes, amphibians, smaller reptiles, some mammals (our ancestors) as well as a variety of plant life and what may be the earliest birds.

It's thought that the dinosaurs may have been competitors of the earlier mammals and many of them (mammals) perished. Some creatures from this period exist today in much the same form as they did then, such as the shark and crocodile/alligator.

As with present day creatures, the dinosaurs evolved to suit a variety of habitats, some eating plants, some eating fish, others eat anything, including other dinosaurs. Some small creatures were confined to scurrying about on the forest floor or in the trees just trying to avoid becoming a meal for one of the larger creatures.

As the dinosaurs evolved they became evolution's highest form of existence (at that time), which is why they were so successful. Evolution is such that some species reach extinction very quickly (on the evolutionary scale), some reach a definitive level and remain there (for example, sharks and crocodiles) and some go on evolving. The dinosaurs were the latter, and so would develop the most intelligence (at that time). They could be compared in many ways to modern-day mammals: some were herbivores; some were carnivores; each species developed differently in different habitats. Some would live and travel in herds or groups, some would hunt co-operatively (much like jackals and lions) and some would be loners.

The most important part of this period is its ending, and the repercussions of this event. After roaming the earth for some 150 million years, the dinosaurs died off. It is still just speculation as to why and how long it took, but it did happen.

One of the most prominent theories, of course, suggests a large meteorite hit the earth sending large amounts of dust particles into the atmosphere, thus producing a climate change, with the predominant plant life dying off. The plant-eating dinosaurs would naturally be the first to go, followed by the rest because the ecological balance was disturbed. If, in fact, the meteorite theory is accurate, that would make *us* a *fluke of nature*, because if it had not happened it is possible the dinosaurs or something similar would still be roaming the earth today, and we humans would not exist.

Evolution gave rise to the dinosaurs, which all began as much more simplistic creatures swimming about in the oceans. These simple water beings eventually moved onto the land. As they evolve, creatures move into, and occupy any habitat that is available, even if this shift requires major biological changes or adaptations, Evolution allows for these important adaptations.

However, the most likely possibility is that the dinosaurs had evolved to a point where they were so highly specialized in their habitats and diet that they simply could not evolve any farther—they had reached the end of their evolutionary path. Perhaps they destroyed their own habitat, much as humans do today. As dinosaurs migrated around the globe because of constant land mass changes, they transferred invasive species from one area to another, much like we do today. The new species would be highly competitive with the existing plants. As the earth continued to evolve, the plant life changed and the dinosaurs could not adapt. Will the current invasive species problems lead to our downfall?

It wasn't until the dinosaurs died off that the mammals were able to expand their territory and move into new habitats, previously unavailable to them. These smaller creatures were probably not as species specific when it came to food and they were not as highly evolved.

The dinosaurs at the time of their extinction were probably producing a limited number of offspring per year, but the smaller creatures were much more prolific, producing many more of their kind in order to ensure survival.

Evolution is based on time and adaptation and so to consider something as unnatural and abrupt as a meteor being the primary cause of such a major change in the development of the earth seems overly dramatic.

* * *

As the climate continued to change and the earth continued to evolve, our little ancestors, as well as some other mammals, continued to thrive. Slowly, at first, and with no other serious competition, they moved out into the rest of the world.

The first land mammals were thought to be small rodent-like creatures. One of the earliest mammals evolving along with, or before, the dinosaurs, may have been more like the present day monkey or lemur. It's a gap that is not completely filled in yet.

Our little monkey-like ancestor could be one of only a few land mammals to have evolved *before* the dinosaurs and outlasted them.

Our little ancestor continues to evolve and spends most of its time in trees. The environment is such that there continues to be plenty of food in its habitat, and so it stays there, for now.

Evolution is a continuous process whereby various species compete for the existing food and space; some live and continue to evolve, and some cannot compete and die. Part of the theory of Evolution is based on *survival of the fittest,* or "the strongest survive". I'm not sure that this is always so, or applies to every species.

Certain creatures will continue to evolve and, much like dinosaurs, become very specialized in habitat and food requirements. While food sources are plentiful, the species thrives, but if there is a change in one or more of its requirements, the species will suffer. If the change is severe enough that species could easily dwindle or even disappear, while smaller weaker species continue to thrive because they can adapt more readily to any changes. So it appears that the species that is of the highest order of evolution is at the greatest disadvantage.

I'd be lying if I said I understand the process of evolution. I don't; no one does. It is doubtful anyone will fully understand the complexities of evolution, and if anyone tells you they do, don't believe them. Society today would be vastly different if even one person completely understood this process.

For the next 40 million years, give or take a little, the mammals rule. Creatures such as woolly mammoths and woolly rhinoceros evolve and thunder about where dinosaurs used to tread. The ocean-going mammals, such as whales, dolphins and seals evolve.

As with creatures before them, nature takes over and a new food web is created. Smaller creatures are eaten by larger ones, plant eaters are eaten by the carnivores and so on.

Plants (flora) also evolve in much the same way as the animals (fauna); various plants become more highly evolved than other plants, with some plants changing very little in millions of years, while others come and go at an amazing rate in evolutionary terms.

Insects have also been around for millions of years and although they do not seem to be changing very much in appearance, they are amazingly adaptable and seem to be thriving despite futile human efforts to eradicate—or at least control—them.

Somewhere along the way the monkeys and the apes took different paths: the monkeys kept swinging in the trees; while some of the apes stayed in the forest, at least one group did not.

HUMANS

At this point I would like to remind readers that, when talking about the human race we must use *generalities* because there are no hard lines or boundaries in evolution.

Our little primate ancestor is quite happy sitting around the forest all day eating fruit. Food is plentiful and the trees offer a measure of safety.

However, the earth is not quite finished moving and changing. Over the course of time seas give way to land, land becomes seas; deserts become fertile grasslands and so on. The existing species adapt or perish.

The climate, depending on where you are, changes quite quickly (in evolutionary terms). Unfortunately for our little ape cousin, their habitat also changes and some rain forests give way to more arid, dry conditions. Open grasslands become more abundant, while rain forest dwindles, and there is less and less habitat to support the population. Adapt or perish.

What happens next is the second most important event in the evolution of mammals after the dinosaurs died off. A group of forest dwelling apes starts, slowly at first, to venture out into the open simply because they have no choice. Now, this just does not happen in one day; it is a gradual process over a very long time. As the climate slowly changes, the primates eventually find themselves at the edge of the rain forest. Slowly, they venture farther and farther out into the open.

This may sound as though they make a conscious choice to do this, but it happens without their even realizing it. Remember this last point because it goes a long way to explaining our present situation. Over time they become more and more comfortable in their new environment, and start to pick up and carry things, such as sticks and small rocks. They discover that when confronted with a larger, more powerful creature they can group together and, with the aid of these sticks and stones, repel an attack, which earlier meant almost certain death for at least one of the group.

By this time, in their evolution, they have progressed far enough to take note of this and remember to repeat it in a similar situation. Once they are comfortable with these new objects, it is just a matter of time until they would be *primarily* used as weapons and tools.

Slowly they learn to forage for anything that looks edible, such as roots, berries and a variety of plants. The human race is on its way to becoming hunter-gatherers. Evolution is a painfully slow process and for perhaps thousands of years these open-terrain primates continue to do this, and to credit our ancestors with any real brainpower at this point I think would be a mistake. They are strictly mimickers or discovering things purely by accident and repeating some of them. Most of their actions at this point are still instinctive.

Many years pass. What happens next is the third and *most important event* in the evolution of humans, and explains our race today. As our relatively docile little ape ancestors go about exploring their new territory, they observe many peculiar things most of which they have not seen before, or paid much attention to when they were back in the forest. As they go about collecting their plants and edibles they notice other *more* aggressive creatures attacking and killing *less* aggressive creatures. As the years go by they continue to huddle in their group and observe the natural carnivores doing what *they* must do to ensure *their* survival, because that is how they evolved.

Eventually our ancestors begin to mimic the other carnivores and begin to use their new weapons, perhaps on smaller creatures at first, or maybe each other much like young children do today.

Over time they become quite good at imitating the other carnivores and since the naturally evolved carnivores seem to show a tremendous increase in aggression at the time of attack, this does not go unnoticed. The only problem with this new talent is that this much aggression is not *natural* for them and so this aggression from this point on is misguided, misdirected, misused and misunderstood. The human race is on a new path.

All during this time, the evolutionary process has been at work, and various species come and go; some adapt and survive, others do not. The tendency is to assume that our ancestor is quite adaptable; however, sometimes the difference between adapting and exploiting can become blurred.

* * *

In his book, Desmond Morris refers to our ancestors as *naked apes*. They were more accurately naked killer apes. People who study early humans have been looking for many years for the *missing link* or a killer ape-like ancestor to try to explain why humans are such aggressive killers and modern apes are not.

In time the carnivore behaviour became our dominant trait and we still remain the top carnivore of the present food chain, despite the distraction of civilization. Other modern day carnivores rarely kill each other.

About the same time, our ancestors were, again unknowingly, walking mostly on two legs, because they had to carry their all-important weapons in their hands. It wouldn't take many generations before this would be considered normal. Eventually the young would not know any other form of locomotion. Over many thousands of years they would eventually walk upright on two legs, and their bones and joints would slowly evolve to accommodate this change.

It is at this point that humans begin very slowly to replace natural instinct with what we refer to today as intelligence. However, one of the biggest problems facing humans today is that *most* humans have lost *most* of their natural instincts and so must rely primarily on learned intelligence. This indicates that education is perhaps the most important influence on human life. Over time we would have to replace natural instinct with *human instinct;* unfortunately not all humans would develop good human instinct, and so end up having very little instinct of any kind.

At this point our ancestors were now herbivores and carnivores; very few other animals could make this claim. They were also changing physically because they were no longer confined to one habitat and a diet of strictly fruit. Their jaws and teeth adapted as they ate more and more foods, which were harder to chew.

Those that left were on their way to becoming present day humans; those that stayed are now the present day gorillas, chimpanzees, orangutans and so on. Don't forget that *they* also evolved from the original primate, which probably looked somewhat different than these species of present day.

Somewhere along the way, millions of years ago, the monkeys and the apes went their separate ways. It was the apes that ventured out of the forest. The question is, did the apes diverge into gorillas, chimpanzees and orangutans before or after leaving the forest? Given that all of these species still inhabit the forests of modern day, we might assume that they had, in fact, evolved into separate species long before *one* of them ventured forth. This leads to the question, which one left? We now know that modern humans and gorillas are virtually identical in skeletal structure and that we share about ninety-eight per cent of the same genes as chimpanzees. My instincts say that a group of ancient chimpanzees are the ones that left. I think that when we look at chimpanzees today, we are looking at our cousins.

As with some other evolving species, *splinter groups* can emerge and go their own way. We know this by observing present day wildlife. As one group becomes too large to be sustained by the surrounding environment, smaller groups break off and form new groups partly because of intense rivalries within the group. Our ancestor had become quite mobile and continued to move out into unknown territory because of their hunter-gatherer abilities. This simple evolutionary event (splinter groups) will help to explain modern human differences later in the book.

Some of the many people who study the origin of early humans are of the opinion that we all originated from one spot (somewhere in Africa), and moved out into the rest of the world from there. Others think that this process occurred simultaneously in several parts of the world, which would, they say, explain the differences in appearance of modern humans (Caucasian, African, Asian and Australian aborigine).

The Out of Africa people suggest that the possibility of such an event happening simultaneously is virtually impossible. This problem appeared to have been solved in 1987 when DNA evidence suggested that we might all have originated from the same female in Africa; however, this finding is far from conclusive, and still unproven.

There are significant gaps in the fossil evidence from various parts of the world and so the debate continues. All of the experts are so intent on being the first human to be credited with such a discovery that they inevitably work against each other, instead of with each other. This appears to be a common trait of most modern humans.

The theory of evolution suggests that the first apes did walk out of the forest somewhere in Africa and after many, many years, a splinter group emerged and went its separate way. This splinter group would go on to become modern Caucasians, Asians, Aborigines and North and South American Indians. The original group would stay in the immediate area and become modern-day Africans.

This second group worked its way out through northern Africa and somewhere in Europe or the Middle East other splinter groups left. Early humans were becoming efficient at hunting and gathering and could—and did—travel wherever they wanted, in random wanderings. At this point their goal was simply to survive, and processes such as reproduction were just something that nature and hormones urged them to do.

Another evolutionary process had been put in motion. Groups continued to travel and separate from here on. During this time the earliest humans would continue to use their sticks and stones, and every so often one in the group would find a slightly better stick or stone and others would benefit (perhaps by accidentally dropping a rock on another rock which would splinter creating a much sharper edge). Slowly, over thousands of years, they would learn to deliberately produce that sharper rock.

Somewhere along the way one of these groups would make its way to what is now modern Europe and become the Caucasian race; another group would end up in what is now China, and from there groups would travel to places like Japan, Korea, Southeast Asia, and Australia. Now, it may sound like there were a lot of groups wandering about, but in fact there were very few, and the world would continue to be very sparsely populated by humans for millions of years, in fact until very recently.

This brings us to another very important point in our history that will help explain modern human behavior, and differences. The major races of people that inhabit the earth today went their separate ways millions of years ago, and have been evolving *separately* all of this time. Although the out of Africa theory is still regarded as the most feasible, the simultaneous evolution theory is not impossible. There are still a lot of unanswered questions, such as pyramids being built by different civilizations at different points in time separated by thousands of miles. This theory is disregarded by many mainly because it is hard to imagine or find any reason or prove that the different races of people would evolve from different apes in complete isolation from each other. It appears on the surface to be illogical that there is no common bond or some catalyst that would create those conditions. Is it possible that one group simply mimicked another? At this point we just don't know, but don't count this theory out.

***

One of the still unexplained mysteries of the human race is how we lost our hair. If we started out as hairy apes, where did the hair go? There are some theories, most of which involve changing climate and surrounding environments, and at this point I would like to add my own theory—I can do that; it's my book.

As the first group left the forest they found the environment somewhat more unsuitable and hostile. One of them discovered, quite by accident, that by lying close to one of their kills, or the kill of another carnivore, that was covered by a luxurious pelt of fur, he or she could stay warm. It would be just a matter of time before all of the group would seek the pelt of any kills. They now, again unknowingly, had reached another important point in their evolution—the wearing of garments for warmth. Anyone who has worked around modern fur-bearing animals knows that it doesn't take long for certain furs to wear or *rub,* as it is called. Modern women who bought long-haired fur coats, such as fox, were usually instructed not to sit down with them on, not even in a car, because the fur would rub. Over the course of thousands of years the hair of our ancestors simply wore off. Over the span of thousands of more years this wearing of pelts would eventually affect hair growth, and hair growth cycles over various parts of the body. It is quite possible that the first women to wear fur coats lived about 4 million years ago. As all of the people of the world today are hairless for the most part, this occurrence probably happened before the first splinter group left and the others simply took that idea with them.

This new phenomenon, combined with the environmental factors, perhaps worked together to relieve us of our hairy coats. It was also at this time that male and female humans began some notable changes in physical appearance, and noticed each other's physical differences.

Sometime during the Stone Age, certain groups came upon areas where there was an abundance of food and a fair climate. They, again unknowingly, stayed in this area longer than they had in any area previously. Because of this they discovered that it was better if only the most experienced of the group went out to hunt game, and while they were out hunting, the weaker members would stay put, in a semi-permanent camp. So far this story has been rather unisexual, but of course there were males and females—families—together in groups. The hunters were mature males who were physically stronger and the ones who stayed back at camp were the females, the young and the very old.

Over the years this arrangement would continue, simply because it worked and because evolution had provided humans with what is known as sexual dimorphism (the male generally being larger and stronger than the female). So, family roles were established thousands of years ago and remained virtually unchanged until very recently. The men continued to go out and hunt while the women stayed at home and gathered, prepared, and cooked the food, and looked after the young. While women were going about their appointed chores, the men lounged around talking about spears.

Over the years more changes allowed for more vocal co-operation. Communication to each other started with simple grunts and a crude language developed. A particular grunt would indicate that one was referring to a particular tool, weapon or person.

* * *

Now would be a good time to explain why men and women today do not understand each other. Back at camp, after a hard day of hunting, the men folk would sit about discussing, as best they could, the day's events. They would grunt to each other what the other did wrong that day otherwise they would have been more successful. Enter the first forms of competition and ego. They would criticize each other, because it is very difficult to admit when one makes a mistake. The women were not allowed to participate in such discussions, only the males. Over the course of time, this social separation would continue and become more and more pronounced. The men would not bother to communicate their matters to the women. Their only communication would be to confirm duties, and so for thousands of years men did the hunting, weapon improvement, and construction and women did mostly domestic chores. One did not cross this line.

Now, in all fairness to men, perhaps the women didn't want to be involved in the men's affairs, and so they stayed apart, except to produce more offspring. This explains why *most* men today seem to understand machines better than they understand women, and women don't understand male thinking.

For more than four million years men and women have evolved *separately together!* Men would concentrate their entire existence and brain development on building a better spear, sword, car, or mousetrap. Women had nothing to do with the mousetrap building but concentrated on raising the young and doing domestic chores about the home. Women today often wonder why men don't think about *them* more than they do; it is because they either can't or have great difficulty because that is the way their brains developed.

One of the physical changes that occurred over time was a pronounced development in genitalia. The women slowly grew larger breasts and buttocks and their facial features were smaller and more "feminine". The males would grow taller and also have larger penises than their ancestors. The reasons for these changes aren't entirely clear. Perhaps as women evolved they lost the biological function of *coming into heat* at certain times of the year and evolution responded by providing features, which would attract a prospective mate, when desired. I'm not going to speculate on the males.

As women walked more and more upright, their hips and pelvic region changed and they would become *biologically* receptive all of the time, and could conceive and give birth at any time. This biological change is somehow connected with our evolution so that we could adapt and survive. The process of giving birth would change. The widening or enlarging of the pelvis would allow for human babies to be born with larger heads. This doesn't necessarily follow right away, but that change would allow further development of the brain, and alter the skull structure.

* * *

Along the way we not only learned how to kill for food, but also ourselves. I'm sure that during those evening discussions tempers rose and one member inadvertently mortally wounded another. An outlaw was born. Group members may have made simple rules and such behavior may have been frowned upon. Eventually the murderer may be cast out of the group. Enter revenge. Generally speaking the members of the group would co-operate and get along.

Hundreds of years might pass before one group stumbled upon another. Enough generations have passed that the current members would not recognize another human if they tripped over them. The two small groups would then either get over their fear and attempt to communicate and exchange ideas, or simply attack and take what the other had. These encounters were extremely rare at this point. Most groups would evolve, mentally and physically, all by themselves, literally for thousands of years without seeing another human being. We'll talk more about this later because it is a key to understanding humans today.

We discovered fire and began to cook a lot of our food, which then was not as difficult to chew, so evolution responded by altering our jaw structure. This event probably happened by accident. Until this point humans made do with roots and plants and it is highly unlikely that they could eat raw meat, but if the raw meat was placed in a fire it make it easier to chew. A new food source was discovered.

So, for the first four or five million years we advanced very little; it is only in about the last 100,000 years that we showed any signs of real self-awareness or advancement.

Some would argue that humans made great strides in intellect, moving from the use of primitive stone tools, to the beginning of farming and the discovery and use of crude naturally occurring metals. However, it is very difficult to give them as much credit as we have, considering that this learning took hundreds of thousands of years to accomplish, mostly by accident or trial and error.

Now we come to the physical change in human development, which will help to explain our entire existence. The *hand* becomes more and more flexible and develops such that it is incredibly articulate and can perform a wide range of simple tasks from the largest to the most delicate. The evolution of the hand precedes the evolution of our brain. While the hand becomes fully evolved, *our brains do not*. We perform many tasks with our hands, which we mistakenly associate with intelligence, or as demonstrating intelligence. Our hands allow us to do things that our brain does not fully understand. Our hands would directly affect the development of the brain. Our hands would give us—and still do—the false impression that we are more intelligent than any other species of mammal, simply because we can physically do things and make things that other species cannot. What most people fail to understand is that the other species of mammals are not necessarily inferior or less intelligent, but because of their evolutionary path, they simply lack the necessity to construct all of the things that humans do. Our hands got the human race to where it is, not our brains. As our hands evolved, they gave us the ability to physically pick up and manipulate objects. This stimulated the brain. Slowly over time, one or more members of the group would discover a better tool or a better way to make a tool, with their hands. This tool, weapon, or household utensil would then be used, perhaps for generations, before another member of the group would have the initiative to try to construct a better one, with their hands. This process is what got us here, and is still in use today.

    I would like to take this opportunity to challenge the reader of this book. In the course of any normal day, observe how often you use your hands, whether you are at home, at work or wherever. Try to estimate what percentage of your activities, whatever they are, involves your hands. Then try to imagine doing that activity without your hands. Try to get through a normal day without using your hands.

***

For thousands of years humans were hunter-gatherers; just prior to the discovery of farming we humans were utilizing many different food sources. Fossil evidence shows that humans ate a wide variety of plants and animals and were tall, robust and healthy creatures. We know from observing modern day hunter-gatherers like the Bushmen of Africa that this lifestyle is not nearly as crude and labor-intensive as we first thought.

Prior to farming, humans may have spent perhaps three or four hours a day doing the hunting and gathering, while the rest of the day was spent back at camp. We may all have done much like the present day Inuit who hunt a seal or caribou, and when that food is gone they go out and hunt another one several days later. This cycle is for the males only; back at camp, women's work never seems to be done.

About 10,000 years ago, someone discovered that they could pull up certain plants from anywhere and stick them in the earth back at camp and some would survive. They eventually realized that if enough plants could be grown beside the camp they would not have to go and collect as many.

About the same time, they discovered that if they could contain or corral one or two of the more docile animals they wouldn't have to hunt them and drag them home. This seemed to be a very beneficial discovery.

Our physical abilities allowed these new farmers to experiment and they eventually discovered that they could plant the seeds of some wild plants and could grow enough right at camp to feed everyone. What a marvelous thing!

What they failed to realize was that by limiting the variety of their foods, and changing their work habits they were set on a path that would result in a steady decline in their health, which still continues today. Instead of eating dozens of different plant species they were now confined to a few. Instead of spending three or four hours a day working, they now had to toil many hard hours a day to sustain their new lifestyle.

What happened here will help to explain our present societies, because this process is still in motion. Instead of going back to being hunter-gatherers, we chose to continue farming. There are a couple of reasons for this: firstly, humans were not intelligent enough to realize what they had done; secondly, once this choice was made and a new evolutionary path was taken it wouldn't take very long for enough changes to occur in their way of life which would make it impossible to reverse—even if they wanted to. Unless a decision of this magnitude is reversed *before* any changes occur, *the new path is set.*

The generally accepted theory on population increase throughout human history is as follows:

Once farming began to increase the amount of food available (however limited in nutritional value), it allowed the group to increase in number. It wasn't long before the population started to increase and so required more food, and as the population continued to increase, so did the food requirements.

This may be the case with a more affluent society, but doesn't explain modern day Africa. It almost appears as though reproduction occurs when humans are their lowest. It could be survival genes coming into play to try and maintain the population or an imbalance in chemicals or hormones because of a lack of nutrition. .

By this time there were many individual groups around the world and slowly the concept of farming would spread to most of them. A few very isolated tribes of people would continue to be hunter-gatherers and still are today.

One of the questions remaining at this point in history is who discovered the concept of farming, and was it a man or a woman?

Which group discovered farming is difficult to say. Men traditionally have been associated with farming throughout history and if you were to observe a modern farm and talk to a modern farmer, he would say that the work involved would be too demanding for a woman. So, did men decide that farming would be easier than being out hunting and dragging food home? I don't think so. I think it was women who discovered farming. The men were totally preoccupied with the concept of hunting and did very little back at camp. The women, on the other hand, were more social creatures and because they were in camp day after day they developed a better sense of awareness and observation and because the gathering part of hunter-gather is more closely associated with farming, it is a short logical step to women—probably older women—doing plant experimentation at camp. Somehow men eventually took over the main farming practices, perhaps because farming evolved in such a way that the work became more and more physically demanding. Perhaps it was only after the men realized what was going on that they thought they could do it better. Some people are like that.

If women had been allowed to continue their new discovery, farming would probably be vastly different today.

* * *

About this time (10,000 years ago) groups were slowly growing and contacts with other groups became more frequent. Some might have been useful and peaceful but most would probably be quite violent affairs because each group was so different in so many respects that communication and co-operation was virtually impossible.

Many isolated groups lacked the intuition or the initiative to take up farming at this point and relied almost totally on either trading or simply raiding and taking what they needed. Enter the first forms of war.

Remember, these groups, which developed into societies and civilizations, have been evolving for hundreds of thousands of years separate from each other. For example, the people of Southeast Asia had not even seen a European or known of their existence until quite recently. It is no mystery why we have such different people in the world today. Each took a separate evolutionary path, and each developed a different culture or society because of their many years of isolation. Each civilization *thinks* differently from the other because their brains *evolved* differently. A European thinks differently than an African, an African thinks differently than someone from the Middle East and so on. The fact that they think differently has little, if anything, to do with intelligence. One is not more intelligent than the others are; they each simply approach life and its problems from different perspectives.

One group may show certain initiatives in some areas and not in others, depending on how they evolved. Some groups would be more aggressive than others. This is one of the reasons the earliest civilizations had a limited life span. As these civilizations developed, the surrounding peoples would want whatever the seemingly more advanced peoples had, and over the course of time they would simply take it during a period of instability. They would then incorporate whatever they liked about the other civilization into their own, setting them on a new path once again.

The earliest civilizations were the first to use farming almost exclusively; that made them stationary and therefore easy targets for more nomadic groups. From then on civilizations or societies would have to try to protect their borders. This, however, was a two-way street and if an empire became too greedy or needed more land to support its growing population, then *they* would be the aggressors and try to conquer and assimilate the surrounding people, or at least to occupy their land.

By this time humans had developed enough self-awareness that some groups were burying their dead. They were conscious of life and death and began to bury certain objects with the deceased; objects that they thought the dead would require on their journey, wherever that might be. Enter superstition. For thousands of years humans could only guess as to what became of that dead person after they stopped moving. Until recently, humans had absolutely no idea where they came from, where they went after they died, or in fact, why they even existed. The idea of burying the dead may have been passed from one group to another but because they all thought differently, they each developed different burial practices and superstitions. These superstitions would often affect the direct development of their cultures for thousands of years.

By this time the different people—Caucasian, Asian, African and Aborigine—were well established, but something else had occurred that would explain many of the problems of today. Caucasian splinter groups would form; Asian splinter groups would form and so on. So, not only were there people who look different not understanding each other, but also now there were groups, which look virtually identical, not understanding each other, or at least not getting along very well. At this point in our evolution, the cultures were developing at a faster pace than they were a million years ago, and so it took only perhaps a few thousand years for a splinter group to develop a completely different path and have a completely different culture or society. The result was people who look exactly the same, but think differently. This will hopefully become clear as we progress through the Roman Empire and Colonialism.

Also by this time humans had made their way to North and South America, between, or perhaps during, one of the many ice ages, and to most of the Pacific region and its islands. These people would develop some of the more interesting cultures because of their isolation and environment.

This brings us to a major development in human history. The peoples of the world would essentially split into two main groups, and each group consisted of many smaller groups. We are going to call these two groups the *Ancients* and the *Moderns.*

The Ancients are all of the indigenous peoples of the world and the Moderns are all of the others and would, of course, develop into what we now know as modern civilization. The Ancients include such groups as the Incas, Aztecs, Mayans, North American natives, Inuit, South Seas natives, Aborigines, Sub-Saharan Africans and so on. These are typically the ones who come to mind for most people. These people would develop on a completely different path from the Moderns.

The Ancients, generally speaking, were calmer, more docile and reflective peoples who, for reasons yet unknown, seemed to be able to blend with their surrounding environment. Despite their initial ancestry of exploiting whatever they could find, they eventually developed cultures that respected nature, the other creatures, and the environment that surrounded them. They seemed to realize how important all of these things were to their survival.

They learned to utilize the surrounding plants and animals without upsetting the balance that kept everything in existence. They realized that many plants had certain characteristics that would keep them—the people—healthy and happy.

All of these groups developed on their own path and each had different customs and individual identities, which distinguished one from the other; combined with their surrounding environment, all developed their own unique culture. The common thread was their ability to harmonize with their surrounding environment.

The Moderns are, generally speaking, the peoples who developed from the Mediterranean through to China, and include such groups as the Slavic (Russian, Pole, Lithuanian, Baltic), Arabic, Turkish, Germanic (modern Europeans), Hindu, Greeks, Romans and so on.

The Egyptians are also unique in that they had what might be considered an 'Ancient' culture at one point but there is no evidence that they lived similar to, say, the Mayans, and so they should be considered Moderns as well.

Interestingly, most of the Moderns stayed and developed from what is now Europe through to China and the Ancients were 'pushed out' to the rest of the world, and so are separate geographically as well as culturally.

The Moderns never seemed to adapt to their surrounding environment. They were primarily exploiters and takers. They relied very heavily on simply taking whatever they needed with no regard for the destruction left behind. They did not blend with their surrounding environment.

This is the area of the world where most of our history is concentrated and also where most of the war, killing and brutality occur.

From this point onward the distinction between *cultures* and *societies* can be made; Ancients had cultures, Moderns had societies. Sometimes people get these confused.

* * *

There is one other evolutionary peculiarity that hasn't been mentioned yet, which helps to support the evolutionary theory—the Neanderthals. This odd group seemingly took their own lonely path. They were less evolved in appearance, yet more evolved in other ways. It is now thought that they were perhaps the first people to bury their dead, as well as place objects in the grave. They showed a remarkable level of self-awareness compared to many others. If we fully understood the process of evolution, the Neanderthals would not be a mystery. They were on a path, which brought them to a point where perhaps they could no longer adapt. Perhaps despite their fearsome muscular appearance they were a more docile, peaceful people who had not learned to kill one another. This certainly makes them more advanced from a social perspective. The surrounding groups would simply be too aggressive for the Neanderthals to survive, and they were perhaps the first victims of conquer and assimilate or genocide. The fact that they were on their own path adds considerable support to the evolutionary theory.

It is difficult to pinpoint the exact time in history when many of these differences occurred, but my estimation is 100,000 to 400,000 years ago—quite recently on the evolutionary scale. At that point in our evolution humans were becoming quite good at killing just about anything, including each other.

CIVILIZATION

Up until this point no humans, neither the Ancients nor the Moderns, made much of an impact on the earth or the environment. That was all about to change. Starting around 10,000 years ago with the concept of farming, and continuing right to the present day, the Moderns would run roughshod over the planet with total disregard for anything except themselves. The main reason for this was that humans were not intelligent enough to realize what they were doing, and the Moderns had not evolved like the Ancients and so continued to exploit. This process is still in motion today.

Despite their differences, a network of trade was developing and so the individual groups (societies) were becoming more aware of one another. For many centuries the groups might trade, or attack and simply take what they could, but they still remained apart. The groups grew in number and each group's population continued to grow slowly. Many groups were now established in a certain area and ventured out only for trading or raiding.

The last 10,000 years of history fill volumes of books detailing the movements of the Moderns as they war with each other, and so will not be repeated here in as much detail. However, many of the main events, which occurred over this period, help to explain modern human behavior and to add credibility to the evolutionary theory. What you are about to read is necessary to provide a continuity in explaining human behavior and our evolutionary process.

Most of us will recall from our studies that the first so-called civilization was Mesopotamia followed soon after by the ancient Egyptians. Mesopotamia was essentially the first society created by the Moderns. It was a small settlement on or near the Tigris and Euphrates rivers, in what is modern-day Iraq. This area was very fertile because of the two large rivers. Records of Mesopotamia's history are still a little sketchy and so it is difficult to say who these people descended from or exactly where they went after their settlement was disrupted, but this is the starting point for what we now know as civilization, and many of the dynamics that occurred here continued for the next 5,000-6,000 years until the present.

History books go to great lengths to make these early societies look very impressive, but in fact most were quite small and simple. The first Mesopotamian society could probably have fit into the boundaries of one modern-day farm (not my observation). Another peculiarity of history books is that they elaborate about these early peoples as though their society was as complex as modern-day society. They talk about the individuals and towns as though the establishment of these settlements resulted from intelligent, conscious thought. Nothing could be farther from the truth. This settlement and many others for centuries to come were random for the most part.

A small group of people stumbled upon a fertile valley and decided to settle there as it provided most of what they needed, and they were essentially left alone for centuries because no one knew they were there. Eventually other small groups of people would settle in the area because of its extensive river system.

From about 8000 BC, when farming apparently was discovered, to 3500 BC when Mesopotamia was settled, the concept of farming spread from its origin (still unknown). To use the concept required going from the more nomadic existence of most Moderns to a permanent settlement. So instead of wandering around and taking what they could from the environment or other nomadic Moderns or having theirs taken, a small group of more enterprising Moderns would settle in one spot. The only problem was that they were now easy targets.

The Mesopotamians began to develop a slightly more complex society than many others. I am not intentionally glossing over, or leaving out these accomplishments because that would create a very biased view of history. The Mesopotamians built some large and impressive temples, and started simple systems of taxation, trade, and writing, and all of these accomplishments are recorded in current books and so need not be repeated here. My objective is simply to provide the *other side* of the story, another perspective of history. Interestingly, the concept of a structured class society emerges here and so I think that it is very clear where this concept—adopted by most Moderns—originated. There was a definite distinction as to who ruled, who the warriors were, and who did the menial labor. So, right from Day One, societies squabbled with one another; there was always one society that wanted to dominate one, or all, of the others. The modern concept, take what the other has, reached new heights.

Mesopotamia eventually split into two major societies, Assyria and Babylon. This was largely due to their system's failure to cope with a major influx of peoples from the surrounding regions.

A new, modern concept was introduced. The groups of people who descended on Mesopotamia were all from different backgrounds and had established their own identities, although most shared the same ancestry. Enter the first clash of different ethnic backgrounds. It is thought that this period records the movements of the Semitic (Jewish) peoples for the first time as they filtered into Mesopotamia in large numbers from the Syrian Desert. The dynamics that followed mixed a large number of different peoples who all had different backgrounds, customs, and opinions; as time went on the concept of *taking a side* would develop. Generally, there were two sides and you had to be on one or the other. Usually these sides emerged in large part to distinguish similarities or differences; the objective became to pick the *winning side*. The Moderns utilized this concept up to and including today. Remember this as it goes a long way to explaining the First and Second World Wars.

From this point onward one of the major objectives of the modern societies was to conquer and assimilate anyone who gets ahead. One would simply take what another society had if they could, an explanation, which may sound a little simplistic, because the circumstances were more complex than that. Usually these takeovers or invasions were the result of the breakdown of trading. Usually one side or the other would simply not comply with what the other side thought was fair or equitable, and so hostilities would develop. There were many reasons why this chain reaction occurred, but the bottom line was that no one knew what was fair or equitable. Remember, it is still basic survival at this point.

The area of the world from the Mediterranean through to Asia would remain in almost constant flux as the Moderns clashed with one another. Except for a period of despotic stability, the Roman Empire, this area remains turbulent today despite the drawing of borders.

Shortly after Mesopotamia came into existence, the mighty Egyptian societies developed. Here again, the earliest settlements were quite small; even at its peak ancient Egypt covered only a small area if measured in square kilometers, but stretched for much of the Nile's length.

Modern scholars have labeled the early civilizations of the Egyptians and Greeks as "ancient" in order to distinguish the periods when they flourished. Although this book may occasionally refer to Ancient Greece or Ancient Egypt, readers should understand the reference is not the same as to *the Ancients*, meaning indigenous peoples.

Egypt presents yet another example of early exploitation. Except for the construction of the pyramids and the sphinx, the history of Egypt is one of almost continuous warfare. Various peoples either infiltrated from the outside to become citizens and find work, while others tried to conquer and take what Egypt had. Egypt also suffered disruptions from in fighting and civil war.

Now we had several large societies with many smaller groups of nomadic people who were continuously fighting among themselves: Egypt, Assyria, Babylon as well as two or three other smaller societies. Until the rise of the Roman Empire, they continued to squabble and kill each other. Out of all of this rose a very interesting dynamic.

The first settlement (Mesopotamia) started to build a stable society for the founding peoples. While they were left on their own, they did very well and a thriving little settlement became the foundation for civilization. Then something happened: other groups of people who had yet to establish their own settlement and were still nomadic with no direction, stumbled upon this oasis in the middle of nowhere, and decided that this might be a good place to live. The Mesopotamians seemed to have a good thing going. There was only one problem. More and more people filtering into the settlement pushed its resources to the limit. Conventional thinking suggests that in-fighting and ethnic tension among the groups eventually caused its demise. Mesopotamia then divided into Assyria and Babylon. From that point onward the Moderns struggled with one another as one society tried to take what the other had. As soon as a society builds wealth and prosperity it immediately becomes a target for others who have fallen behind.

The Moderns have always led this existence, back as far as we can trace their origins. The Moderns have always relied primarily on taking from one another, or from the environment.

Exactly the same thing happened within Egypt itself. The great pyramids were built in the early part of Egyptian history. A group of Moderns settled in the Nile delta because of the fertile soil, and over many centuries they developed an extraordinary ability to build, not only with amazing precision, but also with incredibly large and heavy blocks of stone. To this day it is not known how they did it, and do not expect to find the answers here, but there is one interesting aspect that is consistent with the development of the human race. The Nile dwellers were so well isolated that they evolved on their own, undisturbed for thousands of years, and over that time they developed these abilities. The main building material of choice, especially in this area, was stone: so over many generations they simply refined their building methods, and if left alone long enough, would have perfected these abilities. Eventually other groups of people encroached, or discovered what the Egyptians were doing. Once the original society was disrupted it was never the same; in a relatively short period of time this knowledge was lost, seemingly forever.

The Etruscans, another group of master builders, at the same time were evolving in Italy, and they played a very large role in the development of the Roman Empire.

From this point onward, Egypt never quite regained its glory of the early pyramid dynasties, and it eventually, like Mesopotamia, broke in two. The Upper and Lower Nile empires were at constant war with each other, until the Romans eventually took over.

There were three other major modern societies developing at the same time as Mesopotamia and Egypt: the Indus Valley settlement (India), China, and the Greeks on the Mediterranean. A little later the mighty Persian Empire (Arabs) would dominate most of the Middle East and they will come into the picture shortly. Some major northern nomadic groups who also played a large role later on were developing in northern Europe, the Germanic and Slavic peoples.

Although the Indian and Chinese societies developed into major civilizations and played important roles in the evolution of the Moderns, it is the Greeks, Romans and Europeans who primarily dominated and influenced all of modern development from this point onward.

Before we get to the Greeks and Romans, there is one other interesting aspect of these societies that is worth noting. A disturbing trend was established very early in the history of "civilization"—Dark Ages. Following the collapse of every major society, starting with Mesopotamia, there was a period of instability, war, famine, and disease, which generally disrupted life and was referred to as a Dark Age. We here in Canada are most familiar with the one that occurred in Europe during medieval times, but in fact that was the most recent one and there were many before it. These black spots on history are simply the Moderns struggling to regain some form of stable, productive society after the disintegration of a period of progress.

From the Mesopotamians on, the history of civilization will cycle through periods of relative stability followed by widespread chaos, sometimes lasting several centuries, due to internal and external pressures and an inability to maintain a balance.

The ancient Greeks lived primarily in and around Athens; it was here that the city-state began to appear and became very common throughout the Mediterranean. A city-state was a concentration of people in a built-up area, which began to rely very heavily on outside farming communities to support and supply it. In effect, they were the first urban areas to develop. The city-states were heavily fortified, allowing people to retreat within the outer walls if threatened by their neighbors, which happened quite often.

Very little is known about Greek society before 2000 BC. Despite the fact that the Moderns can account for only about 4,000 to 5,000 years of history, when settlements started to appear, they think very highly of themselves. As a result of a lack of understanding of the concept of evolution, Moderns have a poor perception of time and space. Four thousand years on the evolutionary scale is a drop in a lake, and so Moderns tend to concentrate on the most recent history partly because they don't have much of a history to explore, and partly because prior to this the Moderns were little more than roving bands of barbarians and thugs. It is difficult to accept that as our ancestry.

Greek society finally managed to flourish around 2000 BC as peoples known to us as the Minoans, which developed primarily on the island of Crete. Very little is known about Minoan society, other than the Minoans appear to have traded extensively on mainland Greece. The dynamics, which occurred from this point to the Roman Empire, are almost identical to those of all other developing societies. It is likely that the Minoans flourished simply because they were the first or the earliest Greeks to settle and develop. At some point the group expanded to the point where internal disputes were inevitable and some moved to the mainland, resulting in an intense rivalry. The Minoans managed to hold on for another 200 years or so and then their society went into a serious decline.

The Mycenaean's developed small individual kingdoms on the mainland, which eventually became the city-states of the classical period. Archaeologists have determined that this society, right from its inception, was warlike and entirely geared for war. The prospering Minoans were no match. Evidence further suggests that around 1450 BC much of Crete was destroyed and the existing palaces were burned; the most likely culprits were the mainlanders. From this point onward whatever was left of society would fall under their direct control. It's quite possible that the mainlanders were exiled extremists who staged a coup and destroyed what was a flourishing society and replaced it with an authoritarian, militaristic regime. This was the foundation of modern civilization. It is at this point that the Greeks begin to expand their influence to other parts of the Mediterranean, or in other words, try to take control of as much territory as possible. Mycenaean Greece reached its peak around 1300 BC and then went into decline, finally losing its influence and stability around 1200 BC.

Once again, the same dynamics that were affecting Mesopotamia were occurring here. Greece and the entire area fell into a Dark Age lasting 400 years. There was an unmistakable trend developing—periods of progression and prosperity followed by instability and confusion. After 400 years of a breakdown in trade and a complete economic collapse, Greece emerged on the other side with a new prosperity and the rise of the city-states.

History books do not like to talk much about these dark periods, partly because Moderns are not exactly sure what life was like during a dark age around 1000 BC, but mainly because it reflects badly on Moderns and their history and so a disturbing trend develops. Moderns will grasp any small progression forward and embellish it to inflate their pride and to justify any backward, brutal, barbarian behavior that occurs throughout recorded history. One can only imagine what life was like from 1200 BC to 800 BC in Greece under military despotism. The reason people today are so ignorant and have so much difficulty understanding modern-day society and all of the problems of present day, is due directly to our inability to include the "dark side" of history and to include the bad as well as the good. The result is an entirely one-sided, biased view of our existence. Some humans respond with the attitude that they do not want to, or have to know, the bad stuff and we should only concentrate on the good stuff, or the positive aspects of our accomplishments. That attitude provides only half a story. By ignoring our mistakes we keep repeating them. Maybe, at some point in the future, history will be rewritten, with the whole picture recorded.

From about 800 BC to 431 BC the numerous squabbling kingdoms re-emerged as the historically well-known city-states. Let us not forget who these people were. They were the direct descendants of the war-mongering Mycenaean's and the city-states continued that tradition. The re-emerging city-states had many characteristics of the previously prosperous Minoan society.

The major city-states to re-emerge included Athens, Sparta, and Thebes. These three would skirmish with one another for years without one actually doing a lot of damage to the others. Over time, Athens emerged as the most powerful and progressive of all the city-states. In fact the city-states' intense rivalry, was interrupted by the Persian Empire to the east. During these periods of war with the Persians, all of Greece united temporarily to repel the invaders, and so the groups put aside their differences temporarily.

This system of the city-states, who frequently squabbled among themselves, continued until 431 BC and the Peloponnesian War. Until that period, each city-state essentially developed its own system of governance, however polarized it might be.

What started out to be city states (polis) eventually became fortified city states (acropolis) because, generally speaking, they did not trust each other.

The ancient Greeks were a very organized people who needed to have structure in their society, and are considered the founders of modern governments. They also had perhaps the most clear-cut organized class structure of any society and they made full use of slavery.

The ancient Greek society was such that only mature Greek males had a say in state affairs; women, slaves and all others were essentially property. Over time, the two most distinct systems of governing developed in Athens and Sparta.

The Athenians developed a system that was governed by the people. Greek males, who made up about one-third of the population, ran the state using a "lot" system. This ensured that every male would hold office at least once during his lifetime. The system was quite simple, and there came a point when the society seemed to have reached its peak. It was not until radicals such as Socrates appeared, that the system was challenged. Greek males ran the society; they were considered free citizens, while slaves and women did most of the work.

Sparta, on the other hand, operated in a directly opposite manner. One strong leader ran most of the affairs, and the Spartan men had to answer to this individual. It was essentially a monarchy or republic. Hence the terms "Democrats" and "Republicans"...and two systems that would eventually merge.

Throughout this period it is generally accepted that the Greeks used a system of colonization to exploit many states and cities in and around the Mediterranean. It appears as though after 400 years of instability and confusion that the narrow minded, militaristic Mycenaean's came to the conclusion that they were pretty much useless on their own, and couldn't stand on their own two feet. They began a campaign to conquer and exploit everyone around them. Remember this point, because it goes a long way to explaining the Roman Empire and the British Empire. During this colonization period many non-Greeks from surrounding areas were enslaved in Athens and it became essentially a multicultural society. Not a fair or equitable one, as only Greek males had any rights, but the influx of other peoples and cultures gave Athens the advantage of having an infusion of various ideas and ideologies that the others did not have. Sparta was too narrow-minded to consider such a society, and Thebes never posed a serious threat.

This brings us to a very important turning point for the Moderns, as the most progressive societies in the future will be primarily of multi-ethnic composition.

Despite starting the basis for modern democratic states, the ancient Greek city-states spend a considerable amount of time at war and developing their military defenses. It is interesting to note that virtually all male citizens of Greek society were involved in the military in some capacity. Even as Socrates was being the father of modern philosophy, he was also an officer in the military. Such was Greek society.

Even their "art" was totally consumed by war, as the great vase paintings and reliefs, which historians so eloquently describe in great detail, primarily depict soldiers in battle slaying the enemy. I am not sure they should be labeled "art" but since the Greeks are considered the founders of our modern societies, scholars need to find some splendor in all of the brutality.

Until 338 BC, the skirmishes among the states were reasonably mild affairs compared to what was to come. One state would attack another, frequently at harvest time in an attempt to destroy the other's food supply. The military for most states consisted primarily of foot soldiers (infantry), which would assemble and confront their opponent.

Farmers, landowners, and general citizenry, would grab their armour, helmets, shields and lances, then form up, usually on a level field, and prepare for battle. What happened next could be described as more of a shoving match—a very dangerous one—than an actual battle. The men (hoplites) assembled shoulder to shoulder in rows about eight deep and then advanced on each other, each hoping to break the other's formation. As soon as one side broke, they generally turned and ran, and the battle was over. The rules were that the retreating men could not be pursued or harried and so this type of warfare was used for decades between these rivals. Slowly, over time, advancements were made in armor and its construction and it is the heavy armor with the huge head crests, which defines this period and makes it so recognizable.

We will leave the Greeks for a moment and talk about the Persians as they played a large role in defining the Middle East and North Africa in the not-so-distant future. The Persians were true Arabs. The people of modern day Middle-Eastern countries are mistakenly referred to as Arabs, when in fact most are more Turkish than Arab. When we think of the old Arab societies, with their silks, linens, harems, scimitars, spices, incense and the seductive lifestyle that was associated with it, we are recalling the Persians, and the Persian Empire was great indeed. At its peak it rivaled any other society. When the Persians marched against Greece it was quite a large spectacle, including several elephants, cavalry, infantry, chariots and archers. Despite this impressive display the Persians could never quite overcome the disciplined hoplites and their extensive armor.

The break-up of Mesopotamia left the area unstable and open to invasion. The eventual outcome was the rise of the Persian Empire, as the Iranian people merged with existing kingdoms to form a new society. Because of its unique makeup, it endured many invasions to outlast the Roman Empire (in one form or another). The Persians formed one of the first known religions in history, known as Zoroastrianism, and did not seek to convert others, but were very tolerant of other minorities, customs, and peoples. Despite the insistence of Moderns that the Romans had the mightiest empire, it could be argued that, in fact, the Persian Empire was far more tolerant and enduring than any other.

At its peak it stretched from the Mediterranean to India, and lasted more than 1,000 years, despite periods of instability due to invasions.

Back in Greece the polarization between Athens and Sparta reached its peak in 431 BC and all-out war developed. This period, between 431 and 404 BC, is known as the Peloponnesian War because the area that separated the two was called the Peloponnesus, and this was where most of the fighting occurred. This would prove to be a major turning point in history.

Who actually won the war is open to debate. Modern scholars generally consider Sparta the victor and, if that is the case, the Spartans were progressive enough to incorporate Athenian philosophy. What developed after the war was a mixing of the two societies, although it could be argued that Sparta could have simply asserted its narrow-minded authoritarianism and turned Athens into a clone of itself. At this point, Greek society could have turned into a large dictatorship, but there is little evidence to suggest that happened. So it appears that the war somehow managed to integrate both ideologies, and this is where the basis for modern democracy begins.

For sixty-six years after the war (404 to 338 BC), southern Greece remained fairly unstable as the two major states sorted themselves out. It is quite possible that the Peloponnesian War was the catalyst for the decline of the classic city-states.

During this time there were some other Greeks to the north who, until now, had stayed out of this squabble: the Macedonians. Philip of Macedon's crushing victory over the city-states at the battle of Chaeronia in 338 BC would completely alter history and set the Mediterranean world on a new path. It seems that Athens and Sparta were so engrossed in their bitter rivalry they were unaware of what was happening just north of them, and the Macedonians essentially united Greece under their control.

From 338 BC until the Romans took over, the Macedonians became the overlords of Greece. It was during this period that democracy as we know it was laid out, primarily by philosophers such as Socrates, Plato, and Aristotle.

It was during this period that the basic systems for bureaucratic government, taxation, a common alphabet, science, mathematics, and clearly defined roles for citizens were established. That is not to say that conquer-and-assimilate is a good thing, and that the Macedonians can then take all of the credit for laying democracy's foundations. This society was the combining of all city-states and all ideologies to form the forerunner to modern democracies. The Macedonians were the ones who also laid the foundations for the Roman Empire, and it would not be long before the conquerors became the conquered.

What happened next was one of the most recognizable and talked-about periods in history. In 334 BC Alexander, Philip's son, decided that taking all of Greece was not good enough, so he crossed the Hellespont, which separates Greece from the Middle East, and didn't look back.

What transpired over the next decade is still referred to as "Alexander the Great establishing his empire". Nothing could be farther from the truth. Alexander's actions could best be described as a young, out-of-control, alcoholic bully who went on a murderous rampage. In the court of his father, Alexander's upbringing was primarily geared toward being a leader and a warrior and the reason he is still so revered is because he was a great warrior, but little else. The Romans patterned their empire after this man and his exploits. Think about that as we continue with our young Alexander, who at the age of 20 or 21 was considered to be his father's best military leader and was quickly establishing a loyal following of soldiers. Interestingly, Aristotle tutored Alexander. The riches of the Persian Empire did not go unnoticed by the Macedonians, and as Greek society was now fully immersed in and controlled by money, and the military was entirely financed by money, the Persians and their wealth were very enticing. It is difficult to say whether Philip sent Alexander, or Alexander convinced his father, that they should invade Persia. It is quite possible that Alexander was content to stay in Greece and enjoy his new power. Alexander may have begrudgingly been sent by his father to bring back Persian wealth. Alexander's exploits from here on may have been little more than a disgruntled youth, who was dominated by his father, and at some point during the campaign lost sight of the original intent.

The Macedonians took warfare to a new level. The pushing matches of the hoplite era were gone forever, replaced by a more brutal, complex military that utilized every means at its disposal. Retreating armies were pursued and slaughtered to the last man. The Romans admired Alexander and his fighting techniques. As Alexander pushed farther into Persia, the supply line to his forward forces became increasingly longer and more costly to maintain. It took tons of food and supplies just to maintain his army for one day, and at some point support became impossible. The Macedonian soldiers learned to be more efficient and the concept of the *individual soldier* was born. Each man carried enough supplies to last a few weeks, and it is perhaps at this point that they begin to loose their sense of control from Greece.

Alexander and his soldiers murdered, looted, pillaged and raped until his death in 323 BC, just before his thirty-third birthday. The farther they went, the more costly it was and so it became a vicious cycle as they looted and plundered Persian temples (and then burned them) to finance their invasion. Eventually they had covered most of Persia as well as Egypt. Alexander was unquestionably a very capable and admirable fighter, always at the head of his troops. He was wounded repeatedly and nearly killed several times. Maybe that is why he drank so much. Over several years many of his men rose to prominence as skilled military leaders but at some point, when they were thousands of miles from home, they began to question Alexander and his cause. When they reached India, Alexander was showing no sign of turning back, and his men finally said they were not going any farther, sorry. Therefore, Alexander had to swing around and work his way back toward Greece; at the point of his death he had come almost full circle.

After he was killed, the massive area he had engulfed broke into three major powers. Macedonia proper retained power over Greece; Egypt, with its new capital, Alexandria, established a new dynasty under Ptolemy; the third was the Kingdom of Seleucids. Much of this would fall under Roman control a couple of centuries later. What had been the mighty Persian Empire was thrown into chaos and would never be quite the same, as groups of people established smaller kingdoms, and were back to instability and squabbling. Although it could be said that Alexander the Great was the first man to rule the world, I think it was unwillingly; Julius Caesar is a different story. What Alexander had accomplished was essentially what Genghis Khan would repeat many centuries later, and how it is that Alexander gets to be called "Great" is one of those historical peculiarities that emerge when humans are not quite ready to deal with objective existence.

The Romans soon assimilated whatever the Greeks had managed to accomplish throughout this period. The Greeks had established the concept of modern civilization, with an economy based on precious metals, coinage, and trade, as well as the fundamentals of science, medicine, and law. All of these concepts were being established by many groups of people, but because western democracies of present day consider the lineage of Greek, Roman and European societies to be the foundation for "civilization", any accomplishments outside of these three were either stolen and incorporated by this lineage or simply ignored. As far as the Greeks and Romans were concerned, these concepts (medicine and science) were at their most basic beginnings, while societies such as China were well ahead of the Greeks in these areas.

Again, my intention is not to gloss over any advancement made in classic Greek society. The Greeks, in fact, laid the foundation for modern-day science and medicine, which Europeans would discover and pick up during their "Enlightenment" period more that 1,000 years later. But what is not stressed by history books is the primary reason the Greek men had the time to theorize about life and its complexities, and to establish their god system—women and slaves were doing all the work. I'll leave it to you to decide if the foundation for modern civilization deserves such grandiose attention.

While the Greeks were struggling to maintain unity and get along, there were other groups of people developing in what is now Italy. Oddly, the group that would come to be known as the Romans was not even on a map and seemingly came out of nowhere. There were several other small groups, but the most important peoples to come out of this area were the Etruscans (from the area known as Etruria, now Tuscany). They were master builders, and had quite an extensive society developing, again because of little interference from other peoples. The Romans seem to have appeared out of thin air around 600 BC and were without doubt the most aggressive people. There is evidence to suggest that the Romans may have been Etruscans who separated from the main kingdom and established their own villages, which later formed the city of Rome.

History books state that the Romans expelled the Etruscans in 510 BC and established their own Republic, but it is quite likely that it was the other way around. Oddly, this is almost identical to the Minoan-Mycenaean era many centuries earlier. Given that the Romans were so aggressive and militaristic it is a safe assumption that they were either exiled because of their extreme militaristic aggressiveness, or left of their own accord because the Etruscan rulers would not listen to them. Another disturbing historical trend is becoming well established. The Etruscan-Roman relationship could be compared to the Minoan-Mycenaean or the Athens-Sparta situations. The Etruscans appear to be the more stable, developed society while the Romans ruled their simple collection of villages with a very narrow minded militaristic style. Once again the people who by all appearances are more aggressive (or hawkish) see a more prospering society and for reasons not entirely clear attack and take it over. Is it because the Romans felt that they could make better, or improve the other society if they (Romans) could run things? Or did they realize that they (Romans) were pretty much useless on their own? They eventually regained control over the entire Etruscan Kingdom, and so accomplished by force what they failed to do while they were citizens. This became the beginning of the Roman Empire and from this point onward the military played the most dominant role and everything Etruscan would be called "Roman". From here the Romans continued to assimilate the rest of Italy and its peoples and by 264 BC had complete control.

On the south side of the Mediterranean was another society known as Carthage. The Carthaginians controlled most of North Africa, Sicily, Corsica, Sardinia and southern Spain, and appear to have had an extensive merchant marine and trade system in the western Mediterranean. This implied that they had many ships, and were competent sailors and boat builders. Over the next century Rome and Carthage would fight three major wars, known as the three Punic Wars.

During the second war Hannibal attempted to invade Italy from Spain (218-201) but was repulsed. By 146 BC Carthage and its territories were under Roman control. Impressively, while this was going on, the Romans had also turned east toward Greece and defeated the unstable Hellenistic Kingdoms of Macedonia (197 BC) and Syria (190 BC) and were now virtually unstoppable. A successful war on two fronts was something that Europeans could never accomplish. The Romans now had the builders, the thinkers, and a navy under their direct control and were about to exploit these new acquisitions. There is enough evidence to suggest that the Etruscans and the Carthaginians did extensive trade, and so it is quite possible that the exiled Roman extremists attempted to persuade the rulers of Etruria to take over Carthage and their leaders refused. The extremists then left Etruria probably with the intention of coming back, which they did (my opinion). All of the accomplishments, which are credited as "Roman", came from Etruscan society. Even in the 8th century BC, Etruscan cities had underground sewers and some houses had running water, and the concept of land drainage was conceived there. The Etruscans were using concepts that Europeans could duplicate only in the 19th century AD. They were also apparently good mariners and in 540 BC combined their fleet with Carthage to defeat the encroaching Greeks. They had a type of eastern religion that was founded in and around Babylon and women had equal status in society and could own property. That is not to say that the Etruscans were perfect, as they did consider themselves better than others, employed the use of slavery, and had an odd system of God-worship of which there were many. With all of these societies and their accomplishments under Roman control it is not difficult to see how the unification would be a tremendous benefit to the emerging empire. It was in the early stages of the Roman Empire that the concept of *overlordship* became firmly established. Historians from this period onward refer to all accomplishments as "Roman" because the Romans were in control. All future dictators and potential empire builders would develop and use this concept (for example, the British Empire), and so the conquering peoples are given unparallel status. It is they who are seen as important coordinators, leaders, dictators and kings and so all accomplishments become "theirs", and so it is that quite often it is the most *aggressive* people who dominate from here on and not necessarily the most *progressive* people.

While all of these Moderns, from Greece through to China, were fighting each other for domination and resources, forming confederacies and kingdoms then splitting apart creating chaos and confusion and then forming different kingdoms and so on, there was another people who were almost totally ignored until now—the Celts. Until the Roman Empire began to emerge, the Celtic people were spread across almost all of Western Europe, where they had been for thousands of years.

The Celtic people were unique as they were neither truly Ancient, nor truly Modern. They had somehow managed to become both. The name *Keltoi* first appears in Greek texts around 500 BC referring to the people who inhabited lands on the northern fringes of the Mediterranean. Actually these people did not even call themselves Celts or Druids; the names were inherited from Roman dominance. At their peak, prior to Roman invasion there were about 30 different tribes covering most of Western Europe, each sharing many similarities yet each having its own identity. There are generally considered to be two major centers of Celtic culture, La Tene centered in Switzerland, and Hallstatt in Austria. By 200 BC the Celtic people stretched from the Atlantic Ocean to the Black Sea, and as far north as the Rhine. Over thousands of years the Celtic people evolved producing a very rich, complex *culture* (as different from *society*) combining a balance and knowledge of nature with an affinity for fine metal and woodwork, some of which was so intricate that modern archaeologists were at a loss as to how their findings could have been created. The Celts had a unique and complex burial ceremony and some of the artifacts recovered are of Etruscan origin as well as from other areas to the east, suggesting that the Celts had some contact and perhaps trade with others. Or it could have been stolen spoils.

At the center of Celtic culture was the Druid and Clan system. Again, the name Druid comes from the Romans and prior to that it is not known if the Druids, in fact, called themselves anything other than elders. Despite what people think today, the Druids were not cultist baby slayers that skulked around in dark oak forests. They held special status among the clan elders, and members of the clan consulted them in many of life's matters and because of their knowledge they were greatly respected. This respect and their knowledge stem from their education. The Celtic people did not write down their history as the older Druids committed their knowledge to memory and passed this knowledge to younger apprenticing Druids. It is thought that it may have taken 20 years or longer for younger Druids to learn this knowledge sufficiently to become elder Druids. The knowledge, which commanded such respect was basically the entire history and culture of the Celtic people since anyone could remember, spanning thousands of years, as well as any knowledge accumulated about other peoples. It is this extensive knowledge that has been totally committed to memory that makes a Druid. Standing in Stonehenge today chanting in Gaelic does not make one a Druid.

Thanks to the Romans the Celts are seen merely as war-loving barbarians, but in fact there was more to them than that. The Celts were very much in tune with their environment and lived much like the Ancients in North America. They had an extensive knowledge of many plants and animals that surrounded them and knew which plants and trees could be utilized for nutritional and medicinal purposes. At the center of this culture were trees. The Celtic people greatly revered and respected trees because they were the largest and strongest living things, with the mighty oak being the strongest, and so it was that Druids were drawn to oak stands where they considered the earth's life force to be the strongest. They knew every species of tree and what it could be used for, yet there is no evidence to suggest they exploited the natural resources beyond their needs, or destroyed resources as a result. The land itself was a living sacred entity to the Celtic people. The earth, air, water, trees, animals and even stones were regarded by the Celts as part of the whole. Because they were sensitive to many levels of existence in the world, their life and art reflected both the material world and other worlds of fairies, goddesses, ancestors and spirits. It is this intimate knowledge of all things living that is reflected in their elaborate artwork of swirls and intertwined designs.

There is no doubt that the Celts could also be barbaric and probably did squabble among themselves, but there is no evidence to suggest that one group would attack and want to dominate the others. Most conflict was on an individual basis, with one warrior challenging another for various reasons. The Celts were very superstitious people and the head-severing that they are so infamous for was probably due to their superstitions. Quite often warriors would spend hours cutting off the heads of their enemies to prevent their souls from haunting them later on. Until recently, most of what was known about the Celts came from Romans like Julius Caesar, who often wrote what he observed during his exchanges with them. The only problem was that the Romans, and most other Moderns, were very superficial people who only saw the obvious and did not and could not comprehend the complexity of Celtic culture, which is why the Celts were so badly vilified by the Romans. Even today the Ancient cultures elude the Moderns.

Just to give you a small idea of how much knowledge was lost with the destruction of the Ancient cultures, Julius Caesar once observed Celtic warriors rubbing their own urine on their skin: surely only a "barbarian" would do that. Today if you have a skin affliction or irritation and you visit the dermatologist chances are they will give you a tube of urea cream, which contains similar properties to…you guessed it, human urine. Julius Caesar and others only saw the obvious.

According to Greek records, the Celts and the Greeks did occasionally meet in battle but never to any great extent, and so the easterners appear to leave the Celts to themselves. Before Julius Caesar, the Romans also occasionally did battle with the Celts as bands of warriors occupying northern Italy would strike into central Italy to loot and carry away as much booty and spoils as they could. One famous incident was the battle of Telamon in 225 BC, when pillaging Celts were caught between two Roman armies and were decimated.

* * *

Somewhere between 500 BC and 264 BC the rather small city-state of Rome began to expand its horizons. It took about two centuries for the Romans to control most of Italy. Their main objective was to dominate the Etruscans because without them the Romans were nothing more than extremists and bullies. The Etruscans became the base for the future empire. Between 264 BC and 133 BC the Romans assumed control of Italy, Greece, and Carthage. This included several Celtic tribes, who had occupied northern Italy north of the Po River. All of these people were then given the choice of voluntarily living under Roman law (where the Romans could exploit them) or being sold as slaves.

Until this point the Roman military was content to let the civilian senate make all of the decisions. The senate was formed as the result of Etruscan absorption and by 133 BC had (for reasons unknown) decided to halt expansion of the empire. The Senate then gave orders that unless outsiders provoked an incident, the empire need not expand, and so it appears that from about 133 BC to 58 BC the Roman Empire was happy to stay where it was, and firmly establish the Romans and their laws to oversee their new subjects.

Enter Julius Caesar. To the west were the lands of the Celts (or Gaul as it was named by the Greeks or Romans), to the east the Persians were still holding on to most of the middle east and the Germanic people were beginning to make themselves known north of the Danube River. There is no evidence to suggest that any of these outsiders were a serious threat by themselves, or that they tried to unite and invade the new Roman state. There appears to be a *status quo*.

Most of what we know of the Roman Empire was recorded by the Romans themselves or Greeks under Roman influence, which is why we have such a distorted view of this period. Julius Caesar and others recorded history to *suit them* and painted quite an extraordinary picture. It looks as though everyone fell for it. Ironically, this would set the standard for recording history from then on.

Sometime prior to 58 BC Julius Caesar was born into aristocracy and because of privilege and class worked his way up in the military system to general in command of all western Roman forces. As a general in the Roman military he had many opportunities to observe the Celtic people who had been assimilated and for several years he did his duty and planned his future. In 58 BC he attacked the Celts. Julius intentionally instigated a conflict with the Celts for several reasons. He saw this as a way to control more of the military and gain more influence and power in Rome, eventually gaining more power over the entire empire. Pompey was in charge of the eastern forces and together they would help to expand the empire to its historical limits.

Over the last two centuries the militaristic Romans had been perfecting their fighting techniques and strategies, and once they had combined with and incorporated the Greek military, their knowledge and discipline, the legions were virtually unstoppable. Therefore, despite the direction given by the senate, Julius was about to change history.

At first glance it appears that Julius was a brilliant military tactician because in eight years he had completely destroyed the Celtic culture and occupied all of their lands in Western Europe. Most historians and military buffs consider this as genius, but Julius did have several years to study Celtic fighting techniques and learn everything there was to know about Celtic warfare from assimilated Celts, and so it was not until he was sure he could win that he took them on. Julius also seemed to have something personal against the Celts. We now know that he just made it up as he went along. He recorded many untruths and intentionally falsified his reports to reflect badly on the Celts and justify his invasion. Most of his personal observations were superficial and inaccurate because he simply could not and did not understand Celtic culture and actions. It is quite likely that because of his short stature the taller Celtic warriors intimidated him and my feeling is that he just did not like them. Something very similar would occur many centuries later as the Spaniards failed to understand how it was that a seemingly primitive, barbaric people, like the Mayans could control such vast lands and wealth. The Moderns just did not get it, and the Ancients were about to pay the price.

It is here that historians again run into some confusion and have difficulty dealing with this period. Historians have stated that in 100 BC, a continuous band of "civilization" existed from the Atlantic Ocean to China. This would imply that the Celtic people are part of this "civilization", yet all Roman accounts class the Celts as "barbarians" and somehow subhuman. Historians are not quite sure what to do, so they just move past it and hope nobody notices.

Therefore, Julius continued his conquest of Gaul and along the way he used a concept, which would change history: divide and conquer. This concept was used by many Moderns after the fall of the Roman Empire and is still being used today. Julius achieved this in a couple of ways; one was by tempting some of the clans by offering Roman citizenship and the luxurious, decadent lifestyle that went with it. Some voluntarily came on side, weakening the remaining force. Julius also instigated conflicts to get the clans fighting among themselves. This was not hard to do because the Celtic people, generally speaking are very quick tempered; the British would use the same tactics on the Highlanders of Scotland many years later, and against peoples of the Americas.

On it went until the Celtic people were destroyed and those that remained chose to make their way to Ireland (and possibly Briton), where they could remain free and carry on their own culture rather than become Romans.

It should be pointed out here that, just as the armies of Alexander were paid for their services, so too were the Roman legions. By the time Julius had conquered Gaul and acquired all of the Celtic wealth, he was able to ensure their (Roman soldiers) allegiance with money. The Celts simply fought for their land, pride and honor and their free-fighting techniques was no match for the well-disciplined paid Romans. It is Julius Caesar and his legions that continued to establish the criteria for all militaries to come, right up to and including today.

The Roman legions were primarily made up of "undesirables" or those men who could not succeed as productive members of society. Upon entering service, these men were to declare an oath never to desert their standard, to submit their will to the men who would lead them, and to sacrifice their lives for the emperor and the empire. Regular pay, occasional bonuses (one can only imagine what they were), and a pension upon completion of service did not hurt. Cowardice or disobedience received the severest punishment. Centurions had the authority to have the men beaten, and generals the authority to punish with death. Roman soldiers dreaded their officers more than their enemy. They were then intensively drilled to become little more than robotic fighting machines.

Europeans, such as the British, would employ many of the same techniques; many British soldiers were shot by their own commanders if they hesitated at an order.

This now ensured Julius with control of fully half of the Roman legions. Julius was the first Roman to enter Briton with the intention of also conquering it (when one is on a roll it is very difficult to stop), but his resources were stretched too thin and he could not continue, so he intentionally instigated a fight between the peoples there and then left. This was the man Julius Caesar.

Why he insisted on destroying the entire Celtic culture and its people is unclear, and Julius Caesar himself probably could not give a logical answer, even if he had been asked. He then turned on Pompey and a civil war ensued to see who controlled this new, expanded empire. Julius won. He then returned to Rome (nobody objected) with an extremely powerful and *well-paid* army and assumed complete control of Rome in 46 BC as its first dictator. He was assassinated two years later, presumably by the senators. His adopted son, Octavian (later called Augustus), succeeded him and it was under Augustus that the Roman Empire reached its peak in size, although probably not, as yet, economically or socially.

Julius Caesar was the second man in history to want to rule the entire world, after Alexander. Although it could be argued that Alexander never really wanted an empire.

This changed the entire course of human evolution, because from then on ruling the entire world would be the ultimate goal. What Caesar failed to comprehend was that his achievement was primarily due to the advancements made by the Greeks and Etruscans and because the Roman Empire was then essentially multicultural like the Hellenistic period and not something that *he* had accomplished all on his own, or simply with military force. It was the culmination of everything that preceded it. The Roman Empire was now set on a path that no one could, or seemed to want to, change, and the rest is history, as they say. However, is it?

Julius Caesar almost completely destroyed a culture and its people, which had evolved for thousands of years, and changed the course of history. The Celtic people managed to hold on to some of their culture, such as the language and the individual tartans, which distinguished families and clans, but they were now completely removed from their ancestral lands. This massive disruption caused a tremendous loss of knowledge, which had been accumulating for centuries. Julius focused on destroying the Druid influence and presence because he knew that they were the center of the culture and the source of their knowledge. Once the Druid presence was lost the remaining Celtic people, lacking direction, turned to Christianity. Much of their knowledge about nature was lost with the Druids and they became "modernized".

It was not until 31 BC that Octavian accomplished what Julius Caesar had not and subdued any remaining resistance to Roman domination, with his defeat over Anthony and Cleopatra at Actium. This achievement gave Octavian the unprecedented appointment to "god" status by the senate upon his death, and the right to be worshipped as a god, a lofty appointment for a human. Unfortunately everyone who followed also wanted to be inducted into the god hall of fame.

Once in charge Octavian (Augustus) declared himself as First Citizen (princeps) and. ignoring the senate as his father had, he set about to reshape the existing constitution, set up the government, laws, conquered lands and borders to his design, and only after he unilaterally shaped the entire empire did he allow the senate to share the governing duties. There is no evidence to suggest that Augustus died of anything other than natural causes and he has always been considered the greatest and most capable ruler in the history of the Empire. After his death, the senate was essentially powerless as the ultimate decision-maker was always the emperor.

Under Augustus the empire was at its mightiest, but a succession of emperors who lacked his leadership and his ability to keep the empire stable, would soon cause much concern.

The army was accustomed to being well paid and the person who could keep the military content was given the job, usually due to the death of the previous emperor. The military (generally the Praetorian Guard who surrounded the emperor) simply dispatched the current emperor if they became too disgruntled and appointed someone else. So the job of emperor was a seemingly very dangerous one, yet people wanted it; go figure.

In effect, what Julius Caesar had done was to buy and force his way to power because the system was such that whoever had a substantial amount of money and backing and control of the military had the most power.

Therefore, the Roman Empire was far from being a democracy and despite that fact many people today still consider it very remarkable. The Roman elite viewed *all* others as "barbarians", implying that they, the Romans were very civilized and more advanced, in effect, a *superior people*. What they failed to realize was that this was due to the achievements of the people around them. Thanks to Julius Caesar, the Gauls and many others were painted as somehow "subhuman". The Romans fed people to lions and tigers for entertainment; I fail to see the difference.

The Greeks were the ones who first began to develop the concept of democracy and along the way the Romans rudely interrupted them. So, did the Greeks get a chance to finish what they had started? More on that later.

After Augustus came a series of incredibly bizarre, paranoid and totally incapable successors, with the possible exception of Claudius. The army was choosing the individual who was to be the most powerful man on earth.

The Romans were undoubtedly a very narrow-minded, egomaniacal race that came to power only because of their aggressive military prowess, and their lack of conscience. They totally relied on others to carry them along and to do their bidding and so the Roman Empire was destined for failure right from the start. Despite the special status and position it holds in history, no one can be sure exactly what life was really like during the Roman Empire. Much has been made about the luxurious bathhouses that were built throughout the empire, but life for most was tedious at best. The average citizen lived in fear as Roman laws were executed with severity and brutality and citizens could easily find themselves in the coliseum facing a lion.

Many of Augustus' successors are immortalized, not for their leadership, but for their incredibly brutal and sadistic behavior. Emperors like Caligula, Nero, and many others tortured and killed innocent people and by modern standards would probably be classed as psychopaths. Present day societies adopted much of the Roman model.

Fortunately, while these psychopaths were occupied with their perverse, sadistic pastimes, the Greeks, Etruscans, Celts, and all of the others were running and building the empire, and all the Romans had to do was protect the borders, which they did quite well.

Officially the Empire lasted until about 410 AD, managing to have relative peace and prosperity despite two brief civil wars (69 AD and 193 AD). During this period the Empire was run, according to the "official version", by a civilian government. Many major developments occurred during this time as the Empire introduced a major monetary system, tax system, public buildings, extended the underground sewer concept, built temples, an extensive road system and a shipping network. So, for the first century or so things went pretty well, as everyone was busy building the empire and establishing quite a complicated system of trade, with Rome at the center which reached a population of about one million people. However, several problems began to emerge as the vast majority of the trading was within the empire itself and because of many imbalances in production, the system started to falter.

There appear to have been some serious problems with the movement of goods especially by road, which were expensive to build as well as to use for transfer of goods. As well, several areas were producing only on a local scale while some areas were entirely self-sufficient. The bottom line is that the Empire never seemed to function efficiently and once the Empire was built, the same forces that destroy every major society came into play. The dynamics that *built* the society are different from the dynamics that *maintain* the society. While one is busy building a society there is always a constant, whereby people from all aspects of society are busily engaged in some form of constructive endeavor. For example, roads and buildings have to be built to accommodate new systems of government and the movement of people and goods. More ships are being built because some areas are lacking in certain materials and so the constant to-ing and fro-ing of resources seems unending.

For the first time, perhaps in history, most of the resources required to maintain the society were found within the boundaries of the Empire itself and so there was very little outside trading. There was nobody to trade with. So it appears that the Roman Empire had an inherent flaw in that all of the people who were now part of the Empire could no longer trade as independent nations because they now all belonged to the same nation. The dynamic produced by active trading was then greatly reduced.

The production and movement of goods was very slow and unprofitable and most of the wealth was controlled directly by the emperor, some landowners and other imperial aristocrats. The increasingly overweight bureaucracy and the military became extremely expensive to maintain.

At some point in its development a society reaches its peak and from that point on it becomes almost impossible to achieve the delicate balance required to maintain an empire after it has been built. What follows without doubt is a slow steady decline ultimately resulting in a period of confusion and chaos. Mesopotamia was the first to suffer such a fate.

The Roman Empire was very much like a city-state, only larger. To add to the Empire's internal stresses, there was increasing pressure from external forces. Many of the peoples who were outside of the empire's border were now looking in with great interest.

On the northern border increasing pressure came from a group that had not, until now, been much of a threat: the Germanic people. Occasionally bands of roving warriors wandered south and Julius Caesar occasionally used them as mercenaries against the Celts, but they proved to be highly unstable, impatient, barbaric people and their role was limited. Very little is known about the Germanic people prior to the Roman Empire, and they do not appear to have a well established culture or society. They obviously had some knowledge of metalworking as they had a variety of weapons, such as battle axes and swords. Despite this, they still appear to be quite primitive compared to other peoples. Even the Celtic warriors were shocked at their first encounter with these incredibly brutal, animal-skin-wearing, sword-swinging behemoths, but the rivers (like the Danube) provided natural, easily defended borders, that kept them at bay. They obviously wanted what they themselves did not have, which was everything. They will come back into the picture shortly.

Back in the Roman Empire, the Greeks were teaching the Romans about gods and politics. The concept of *rhetoric* was expanded under the Romans and taught to all the young Roman aristocracy as part of their tutoring. Rhetoric was defined at the time as *the art of speaking without actually saying anything.* This somehow seems appropriate for modern societies as this concept is still in use today.

The Romans were pagans who worshipped many different gods; at one point they had in excess of 200 deities. There was a god for everything from war to simple household duties. The Romans incorporated many of the Greek gods with some existing Etruscan gods and the Romans even considered themselves as gods because all of their gods had human form and so they unrealistically aspired to achieve this supreme state, adding to their already delusional behavior.

The Greeks, Romans, and others established and worshipped their gods primarily because they had not evolved far enough to be aware of conscious thought; in other words they functioned as though all of their thoughts came from one of their gods and did not know that it originated inside of their own minds. This will be expanded upon when we reach The Enlightenment.

Another major Roman development was the increasing importance placed on material wealth. During the Roman reign material possessions were considered to be more important than human life.

Any Roman who held citizenship (officially granted by the bureaucracy) who caught, or even suspected, someone stealing from him had the legal right to kill that person on the spot or have them executed. Roman males had absolute authority over their wives and children and had the authority to have any or all of them executed or sold into slavery (occasionally for a variety of seemingly insignificant offences).

Among the Greeks several prominent people stand out in history, and their philosophies are still studied today, showing that the Greeks were at least trying to comprehend what life was. The Romans totally lacked this ability.

Another one of the internal pressures that would play a significant role in history from then on is religion. The first of the "big three" (Judaism, Christianity, Islam) to enter the scene was Judaism. The familiar story tells of Moses, the Jewish peoples and their exodus out of Egypt to escape oppression by the Pharaohs. It is thought that many Jews may have unwillingly participated in the construction of at least some of the pyramids. The story goes that Moses didn't realize he was Semitic and when he found out, he then led his people to freedom where they wandered for many years in the desert until settling in Jerusalem. Exactly how and when they came to be enslaved in Egypt is unclear as is the exact date they settled in Jerusalem. While they were wandering, still under the guidance of Moses, he made his famous journey up Mount Sinai, where he encountered God for the first time. After many days he came down and spoke to the people of his divine revelation and explained to them what, essentially, would be the beginnings of Judaism.

He told them that the suffering they had endured at the hands of the Egyptians and consequently the suffering they had then, in the desert, in the middle of nowhere, was for a reason. He, Moses, had spoken to the one almighty God, who was responsible for creating man, and all of the other natural things that surrounded them. God had spoken to him and told him that the Jewish people were the "chosen ones" and they, and they alone must carry the burden for mankind. He continued by saying that only they could serve this one, almighty God, and that they should go forth, multiply and show obedience to divine commandment. At some point after this the Old Testament of the Bible was written to lay the foundation of Judaism. No one knows if it was written by Moses himself or by another person or persons.

The basis for this faith was *God is*. That he is does not have to be proved. All creatures and things that are, are his will, and the sun shines and nature exists because he wills it. Over time, like all religions, this faith or belief would be expanded and further defined by followers.

Judaism, as do many other religions founded by the Moderns, believes that there was a definite starting point for man and the earth and that there will be a definite ending point. God, it is said, does not have any positive attributes, and that any negative attributes are simply to direct man toward the truth. This is one way of explaining the evil of man, or the evils that men do. If men commit acts that are not "moral", this is how God is showing man the path to truth.

Judaism does a very good job of defining how all living things live in harmony and balance but, as opposed to the theory of evolution, the Jewish people have believed, and continue to believe that he guides all of this.

At some point in history Rabbi Akiva and three others are said to have "ascended to the highest firmament, that of God." Only Rabbi Akiva came out unharmed (the others were destroyed) and so the concept of *Rabbi* was introduced. Throughout history there would be several notable Jewish prophets, such as Maimonides, who is considered the paramount authority of Jewish law, but even he was occasionally questioned.

The written word of Judaism is the Torah, the Bible (Old Testament) and the Talmud. The Jewish people were essentially the first to believe in one god but they also believed that only they could believe in God. Over time the Jewish people, because of centuries of persecution, were at odds as they struggled to balance their belief, that they were, and are, the "priest people", and keep themselves separate, and yet wanting to be part of society as a whole. Throughout history the Jews continued to live within societies dominated by non-Jews with their belief that they were the chosen people, a belief that inevitably would draw criticism, at times quite severe.

Jewish law dictates that all Jews are a brotherhood, and that if the Jewish people of one part of the world ask for help then other Jews are obliged to offer assistance.

One of the fundamentals of Judaism is the belief that a messiah will appear to walk the earth as a man and that this individual would be sent by God, to guide them. This would lead to one of several major disagreements among Judaism, Christianity, and Islam. The Jewish people believe that the messiah has not come yet.

Did Moses actually speak to his god, or was he simply a well-educated man who offered some hope to the people following him, when there seemed to be very little hope?

Back at the Roman Empire and Jerusalem there were several groups of Semitic people, some of whom were considered to be more moderate while others were more political (zealots), each hoping the messiah would liberate them once more, this time from the Romans.

The Romans tolerated many cultures and beliefs as long as everyone obeyed Roman laws, which weren't all that democratic. Generally speaking, if you weren't Roman your life rested precariously in the hands of the regional procurator. One of the main reasons that the Romans allowed other cultures was their own ignorance: they were fascinated by and curious about other people and what guided their lives. They stubbornly held to pagan guidance, but it was obvious they were easily confused because of their profusion of gods of which a new one could be added at whim.

The Jewish people were now spread throughout the Empire in small pockets, and were exploited and heavily taxed along with everyone else. They went about their lives doing their best not to upset the Romans and to maintain their beliefs, always knowing that the messiah would come.

Enter the Messiah. Somewhere in one of those groups in Jerusalem there lived a man who was about to change history. For the first thirty years of his life Jesus Christ was pretty much like every other Jewish person, at least to the casual observer. At the age of 30 he began to preach the very message that the Jewish people had been waiting for, "the Kingdom of God is at hand."

It is now generally thought that Jesus came by his religious thoughts via another man called John, the Baptist. John was thought to be the first to tell people about the messiah's impending arrival, and sometime after the Romans put John to death, Jesus took up his cause. John's message, carried on by Jesus, stated that there was definitely one almighty "God," who was going to make himself known in the not-too-distant future. The other Jews began to show interest and many believed (or wanted to believe) that he was genuine and that he, Jesus, was the messiah that they so desperately wanted. However, over time Jesus' message began to change; he then said that God was not necessarily going to liberate the Jews alone, as they had hoped, but instead was going to liberate all men. He said that all men were created equal and that all men, Romans included, could serve God, and that God was not just for the Jewish people. Needless to say, the Jewish people were not overly keen on this idea.

Despite their withdrawal and growing resentment of Jesus, the concept began to grow and Jesus obtained several followers. Within a relatively short period of time, Jesus and his new religion found support in many urban areas throughout the Empire. The other Jews saw Jesus as a threat to their beliefs and so they conspired to turn Jesus over to the Procurator and he was crucified. Initially many of his followers abandoned him, but their faith was restored when, they say, Jesus appeared to them after his death (the resurrection) to proclaim God's supreme power.

.   It was only after his death that the concept of Christianity spread because of his disciples and their renewed faith.

It is difficult to say if John told Jesus that God considered all men equal, or if Jesus maybe added that himself later. John may have simply been trying to convince the others that there was hope, or that he, John, was their messiah. However, Jesus Christ was considered to be "the Messiah" by his followers and the idea grew.

Perhaps Jesus thought he could convert the Romans, as this would certainly make life a lot better, because as it was, life was generally wretched. If he could convince everyone that God saw them all equally and that in his eyes they could all benefit from his glory, then everyone just might get along. This was historically the first real test of Judaism but the Jewish people did not consider Jesus to be the messiah and so held to their fundamental faith. This snubbing and the subsequent death of Jesus Christ would forever cause friction between Judaism and Christianity. Likewise, the Romans considered this new phenomenon to be a nuisance and persecuted many Christians. Unfortunately most of this persecution was occurring under the emperor Nero who was unstable on his best day, and many believed that he used Christians as scapegoats to divert attention away from his peculiar irregularities and poor leadership.

Jesus and his message appealed particularly to the poor and humble, who saw some kind of hope and salvation in an otherwise brutal world: the seed had been planted and was now unstoppable. By 600 AD Christianity would encompass the entire Roman Empire, and even some outsiders such as the Germanics were influenced by it.

Jesus, of course, did not know about dinosaurs and the theory of evolution. Despite that, his religion, and in fact, all of the religions show a remarkable degree of insight into human nature, which is the main reason they are still followed today. At its time of inception, each religion is a reflection of basic human nature, and one religion is not necessarily better than the others, just a little different. In fact they are all very much the same and share much more than they are willing to admit; we will discuss that a little later when Islam enters the picture.

From 235 AD onward the Empire fell under direct military control; until Rome was sacked in 410 AD it was essentially a military dictatorship. Internal and external pressures were creating tremendous problems and had it not been for a series of strong emperors from 268 to 284 AD the empire might have collapsed. In 284 AD Diocletian came to the conclusion that one emperor could not control the entire Empire and he subdivided it into four prefectura, one being a joint Augustus equal to him while the other two were subordinate Caesars. Shortly after this, the sphere of power was shifting to the eastern capital of Byzantium, later called Constantinople.

The tax system was revamped and provided a temporary revival but the only thing holding the Empire from being overrun was the rather persistent and well-disciplined military. Slowly the outer ring of the Empire gave way to increasing barbarian pressure and when Constantine officially moved the center of power from Rome to Byzantium in the late fourth century he pretty much sealed the Empire's fate. Constantine later renamed the city Constantinople (The Romans were so humble), and even converted to Christianity.

In 410 AD the Visigoth, Alaric, overran Rome and in 455 AD the Vandal, Gaeseric also sacked Rome (both

Germanics); an Ostrogothic kingdom was established in Italy by 493 AD.

During most of its existence the Empire was becoming increasingly polarized between the rich and poor, and in his extensive work, *The Decline and Fall of the Roman Empire,* Edward Gibbon makes several references to the economy of the time, and how brutally excessive the tax burden became to the citizens. The rich seemed to be getting richer and the poor, poorer (sound familiar?). Much of the eastern half would remain intact and continue with Roman law and authority, but eventually Greek would supersede Latin and the Roman influence slowly diminished. Justinian would attempt to reunite the two halves in the mid sixth century, but to no avail. At some point the emperor was not even Roman, but the descendant of one of the conquered and assimilated outsiders. Ironically, but not surprisingly, it would be non-Romans who would keep the eastern half alive for another 1,000 years until it was overrun by the Turks in 1453.

The west had a very strong Christian following and the Roman Catholic Church was well established even before the final collapse of the Roman Empire. Apparently its structure was patterned after Roman bureaucracy and the clerical elite were the bishops.

What happened next would change the course of history yet again. The Western Empire crumbled, setting in motion a very large movement of various peoples around the once mighty empire and groups (primarily of nomadic nature) rushed in from all sides to fill the void. The Huns, under Attila, came from somewhere in the far east, the Germanic peoples crossed the Danube, the Berbers and others invaded from Northern Africa, and the Slavic people came down from the northeast (what is now Poland and

Lithuania). This sudden influx of people destroyed whatever was left of the Western Empire and disrupted the entire area. At this point the Romans just seem to disappear. But did they? Where did they go?

Over the next 1,000 years Europe was the most backward area of the world as these barbarians struggled with each other.

About the same time the Angles and Saxons were looking toward Briton, and would establish some settlements on the eastern side and remain there until the Normans arrived in 1066. All of these groups of people (the Normans, Angles, Saxons, Goths, Visigoths, Ostrogoths, Vandals, Franks, Jutes, Allemani and Burgundians) are of Germanic descent and all share the same ancestry. However, at some point they separated, and although they shared the same background, they began to develop their own identities.

The Roman Empire was not forgotten as most of these groups had been on the border of the empire, looking in, for many years. Some of these groups would become modern European states based on the Roman system, many centuries later.

Through the Dark Ages and Middle Ages these groups struggled to form some type of structured society, similar to the Roman Empire. I say struggled, because the structured society that the Romans had established (with the help of others) was foreign to them and they did not have any other example to follow, and greatly admired the Romans and their exploits.

Most of the societies accepted Christianity and the Roman Catholic Church was well underway as the only institution with any form of structure. This Church essentially ruled Europe for the next 1,000 years until King

Henry VIII of England wrestled control of the state from the church with Protestantism. So it was not until around 1500 AD that Germanic peoples were able to form the rudiments of a democracy and separate from the church.

Up to the point where the Empire reached its peak, the Romans and everyone else were occupied with the actual building of the empire and so everyone had a focus or function. Once the Empire was established it became a rather mundane task just to maintain it and protect its borders. Perhaps it was at this point that the Romans simply did not know how to make the adjustment as they seemed to be naturally aggressive and their entire existence seemed to rely on maintaining that aggression.

* * *

The main cause of this enormous movement of people was the Huns. Mid-way through the Roman Empire, a build-up of primarily nomadic peoples from central Asia, moved toward the Empire, as well as toward India and China (other centers of civilization). A whole multitude of nomadic groups, too many to mention, were set in motion and either were pushed ahead of, or followed behind the Huns in the early fifth century. Apparently it was the Huns who drove the Germanic people across the Danube and into Europe, then to the Mediterranean and even as far as North Africa. The Slavic people were moved from the north to Eastern Europe and the Balkans and, by the end of the eighth century, Croatian, Serbian, and Bulgarian states were forming.

From the demise of the Roman Empire until well into the second millennium, the entire world as it was known was thrown into absolute chaos as various groups of Moderns were at war with each other for control of what had been a reasonably stable existence from Europe through to China. Many of the nomadic groups who had sat on the outside looking in on civilization around the Roman Empire, as well as India and China, came rushing in, not realizing that their actions would cause such massive destruction and disruption. Only China was able to successfully hold off this surge of people.

Once again the dynamics that had shaped the Moderns since Mesopotamia occur, but on a much larger scale. People who were shut out of the rich neighborhood, as it were, wanted to come in and benefit from what others had done (by force if necessary). The large numbers of incoming people were too much for the societies to absorb and a weakening state would be totally overcome as a result.

During his attempt to reunite the Empire, Justinian sent his general, Belisarius, against the Huns; with the death of Attila in 453 AD the Huns retreated to the Russian plains.

Europe was then being reshaped by primarily the Germanic and Slavic peoples and remained the darkest and most backward part of the world for centuries, because of their unstable barbarian ancestry.

* * *

During this rather turbulent time, there arose the last of the big three modern religions, Islam, somewhere @ 768 AD (depending on which book you read) founded by Muhammad. Hinduism and Buddhism were primarily centered and isolated in India and China and therefore did not play as big a role in the development of the Moderns. The big three were far more aggressive.

Islam is an integrated way of life. The Muslim (one who submits) lives face to face with Allah (God) at all times: there is no separation or intervention between his life and his religion, his politics and his faith. There is a strong emphasis on the brotherhood of men, co-operating to fulfill the will of Allah. A Muslim lives to serve God.

The Quran is the word of God, and God has spoken to man in the Quran (written down by Muhammad). Muslims have never questioned that these words are true. In Muslim scripture the story of the Garden of Eden is very much like the Judeo-Christian "Genesis"; however, Muslims do not view Adam as having committed a sin for which all men will atone but is viewed as having committed an error in judgment. Adam was the first prophet, because he was the first to whom God revealed himself. After Adam came several more prophets who corrupted the word of God, and so God sent Muhammad with his final revelation to set out his word in a definitive form which would not be lost.

Moses is also considered a prophet who was sent to rescue the children of Ishmael's nephew, Israel, from Egypt. It is said that afterward they considered themselves to be the chosen people and in doing so disobeyed God and betrayed their brethren. Jesus Christ is also considered a prophet through whom God spoke. Born of a virgin, he is highly praised in Islam; however, Muslims believe Jesus did not die on the cross, there was no atonement or resurrection and he was not the son of God. It is said that Christians falsified the scripture and the word that Jesus brought and so they have been blasphemous.

Abraham, who was of Jewish ancestry, is viewed in the Quran as being the quintessential Muslim. With his son, Ishmael, he built the Temple of the Ka'ba (Mecca) and instituted the rites of pilgrimage. The Quran says that because he submitted himself to God he was a Muslim, and does not belong to Hinduism or Christianity, although all three religions claim him.

Whenever men found themselves straying from the path or the word of God, and were generally corrupt and perverse, they had a "new revelation", which was God speaking to them.

From 768 AD to the late fourteenth century there was no prophet or spiritual leader after Muhammad. A historian Ibn Khaldum, who was considered to be a direct descendant of the original Arab Muslims prior to the Mongol invasions, wrote a book in which he declared that from that point onward, any ruler who ruled "Islamically" is considered a successor to Muhammad.

Muslims do not claim direct association with God because God is unknowable, but follow his last words (Quran) with unquestioned devotion and service, unless he chooses to reveal himself.

Since men could not physically see God they had to rationalize his existence somehow. Throughout history they set down scriptures and revelations in attempts to describe God and to justify his existence. This becomes confusing in all the major religions, as they can only consciously envision God as being like a man because they have no other example to envision, yet he then becomes an all-knowing being who is not a physical being. One thing they are sure of is that he is only one or in other words one being as opposed to two or more. On that much they agree.

Over the course of history each religion continued to change and shift, sometimes straying from its original path and sometimes returning. It was difficult for the men of all religions to hold to the original path as time went on, because from the time of Moses, Jesus, and Muhammad, men were essentially on their own; from that point onward many different interpretations emerged and some were kept, while some were rejected.

Over the next 2,000 years each religion would produce several different factions from extremists who tried to hold to God's word as it was interpreted by the first prophets, to those who see religion as outdated dogma.

The big three religions started essentially from the beginning with religion and religious law and attempted to maintain that as a main focus, whereas the Greeks and Romans developed systems of law prior to converting to a religion or being exposed to these religions. Even though the invading Germanics adopted Christianity when the Empire expired, they were greatly influenced by the empire and its structure and so the concept of having state laws and religion was mixed together at that point.

At some point all of the religions began to expand on the original scriptures and much of this writing was dedicated to setting out in writing how men must act, how men should treat all others around them, even giving specifics as to relatives, spouses, offspring, neighbors, friends, enemies and even animals.

All of this was essentially the Moderns having to *consciously establish* their morals and values because, unlike the Ancients, they did not *evolve* having these characteristics naturally embedded in their makeup.

Christianity and Judaism both have an official "Sabbath" or day of rest, because God labored and then rested. How they know that God rests is still a mystery to me.

God was also not created, as he has always existed, and he created all things living, a belief similar to the present theory about the universe, whether it was created or always existed. Perhaps they are one and the same.

Muhammad was quite right when he said that Christians perverted the word of God. The Germanic people had limited exposure to the concept prior to the collapse of the Empire. So what developed was a race of barbarians who never had a developed, stable society continuing Christianity after its inception.

Christianity was developed by barbarians, Muslims took what they wanted from Christianity, and Judaism put a different slant on the whole thing with the Jewish people thinking that only they can serve God. Quite a dilemma.

So all three religions share the same God, all three share some of the same prophets, all three have the same base for their beliefs. It appears that the main conflict between them is who—which human or humans—will convey his word here on earth. I have come to the conclusion that the problem lies not with the religions and their basic common link (God), but with the humans who try, but fail, to follow it.

MORE CIVILIZATION

It was during the Roman Empire that the Jewish people were uprooted from Palestine and spread throughout the empire. This was the result of two large-scale revolts the Jewish people directed at the Romans in an attempt to break their control. The first was 66-73 AD when a rebellion forced the legions to regain control and destroyed the main temple in Jerusalem. The Zealots held out longer at Masada but were eventually overcome after a lengthy siege.

The second revolt, 132-135 AD, caused irreversible damage to the area and resulted in the dispersal of Jews all across the empire, from the Middle East to Spain and north into Gaul and the Rhine.

It was here that the Jewish people began their long and desperate struggle to retain their identity and their religion while living within other societies. These smaller communities would lay the foundations of a more decentralized faith with the development of the synagogue, rabbinical and communal prayer.

The Jewish people would face persecution and expulsion from this point onward, primarily by Christians, with the "final solution" coming in Nazi Germany.

After the breakup of the Roman Empire the entire world (as it was known) from Europe through to China became polarized between Christian Europe and a very rapidly spreading Islam. By the middle of the ninth century, Islam had spread to most of the Middle East, east to the

Punjab, all of North Africa and into Spain. This polarization would result in centuries of brutal conflict based primarily on how one worshipped God.

To some this may seem somewhat ludicrous now, but at the time it meant the very existence of man. Whenever you read history, you should at least try to put yourself there, in the year 482, 532, 814, or 1066 and try to imagine what the people of that period thought or how they perceived life. At those points in history and, in fact, until very recently, humans had very little knowledge about anything except war. The Moderns simply could not grasp the same basic fundamentals of life that the Ancients had evolved with. From the fall of the Roman Empire until the twentieth century, the peoples who took over were nothing more than total barbarians. Western Europe was conquered and settled primarily by the Germanic people who, although they accepted Christianity, knew nothing about "structured society".

They came running, swords swinging, into a Roman ghost town and the only thing that they found was the Catholic Church, and a lot of cities, buildings, and roads that they had no idea what to do with. The Etruscans had running water and sewers in 800 BC and Europeans simply couldn't grasp these fundamentals, as European cities were incredibly backward and primitive until quite recently.

When they took over from the Romans it was the Catholic Church that had to show them the most basic aspects of everyday life, and for centuries Europeans knew nothing more than how to write and record simple daily events as they unfolded.

Over the course of European history many men would try to recreate the Roman Empire but could not succeed because they didn't understand the same concepts that the Greeks and Romans did. As a result Europe would develop a simple system of kingdoms and monarchies trying to assume the absolute authority of a Julius Caesar or an Alexander.

The first major power block to come out of the Germanic invasion was the Frankish Kingdom which lasted from about 480 AD to the mid-800s. For about three centuries the Franks dominated Europe due to the success of Clovis and his sons around 500 AD; their domination ended with the decline of the Carolingians and Charlemagne.

During this period the Franks pushed out some of the other Germanics and conquered and ruled by force all of the others. It would be this period that would lay the foundations for a long and brutal rivalry between the Britons (English), the Franks (French) and the Burgundians (Germans).

Interestingly, the concept of "what goes around, comes around" would catch up with the Franks many centuries later as the English and the Germans would ally with each other many times in an attempt to subdue France. For centuries these three would struggle with one another for control of Europe, ending in the two most brutal conflicts in history, World Wars I and II.

With the death of Charlemagne in 814 AD the Carolingian Kingdom disintegrated within about 30 years. The result of a lack of real structure or major cities, allowed individual nobles and knights to seize local control and the "feudal system" was born, based on simple peasants working the land and paying brutally oppressive taxes.

The Frankish Kingdom was broken. For many years—centuries—the Franks and the Germans would manage to retain this part of Europe despite invasions from the east and fighting one another. Europe would be broken into many smaller centers of power and would remain backward, disunited, and unstable until the rise of the more modern nation states.

* * *

Once the Carolingian Kingdom was in disarray it was vulnerable to invasion from all sides, and didn't have to wait long for this new onslaught. The Germanic people now found themselves trying to defend what they had taken from the Romans.

In the ninth and tenth century three groups of people appeared who, although they made themselves known, did not have a major impact on the world as a whole. However, each major movement of people changed the dynamics or makeup of an area, sometimes very subtly, sometimes in more important ways.

The Saracens (Muslims) invaded Europe from North Africa, and had some influence in southern Spain, southern France, and Italy.

The Magyars came from Eastern Europe, destroyed the small Bulgarian Kingdom that had been forming, and caused disruption as far west as Paris.

The most notable of the three were the Vikings. At that time Scandinavia was essentially the Norwegians on the west coast, the Swedes on the east coast and the Danes, who originated and remained in what is now Denmark.

The Norwegians were excellent boatmen and the long-boat is famous throughout history as being perhaps the most versatile boat ever built. Although their reasons for these historic voyages are somewhat unclear, one can assume at this point that they were doing what everyone else was, which was to take as much from others as one could.

They appear to have been primarily coastal people, not overly interested in going anywhere that their boats could not go. They took their long-boats up a river as far as they would go and seem to be satisfied at that, and so the Scandinavians appear to have evolved around the sea and their boats.

The Norwegians and the Danes would have some impact on the development of Britain and Ireland.

* * *

Before we get to those, we should talk a little about what was happening in Britain (at some point Briton became Britain). The history of Britain is incredibly long and complicated, so don't expect to have it all explained here and now because I still don't know the history in great detail. However, there are some major events, which shaped the development of this area.

After the destruction of Gaul and the ancient Celts by Julius Caesar, many Celts made their way to Ireland and southern Britain. These people would be the ancestors of the Scottish, Welsh, and Irish of the present day. They would adopt Christianity and would become very devout Catholics until many converted to Protestantism.

Sometime during the early part of the Roman Empire a group from Ireland known as the "Scots" made their way to northern and western Britain. There they encountered a people who came to be known as the "Picts". No one knows where the Picts came from, whom they were, or how long they had been there, and it was either the Scots, but probably the Romans, that gave them the name *Picti.*

The Pictish people are a total mystery, but it is obvious they were one of the first inhabitants of Britain and rightly considered it to be theirs. It is thought that they were divided into two main tribes, the northern and southern Picts.

Somehow, the Scots and at least the northern Picts joined, or integrated, and for many years repelled Roman advances into what is now Scotland.

In 404 AD when the Romans officially pulled out, the Angles and Saxons (Germanics) invaded south-eastern Britain, and for the next 500 years the Scots, Picts, Angles and Saxons were at constant odds with one another, with no one group really asserting any unification or absolute control over the entire island.

For many years the Picts resisted the invaders and somewhere along the way they became assimilated into the peoples of Scotland.

The Angles and Saxons fought for control of southern and eastern Britain for many years and slowly began to merge the people south of Hadrian's Wall, built by the Romans. It was during this period that Celtic and Anglo-Saxon identities begin to blend in the South. Sometime in this period the legends of Arthur and his knights emerged and are immortalized in British history. Although the present day English touts Arthur as *theirs,* there is now enough evidence to show that Arthur may have been, *Celtic,* but was heavily influenced by the Saxons and their way of life. Another theory says he came from somewhere in the east. Arthur appears somewhere either near the border between England and Scotland or in Cornwall in the southwest, and was neither a true Saxon nor Scot but has formed a separate identity as he comes to be known as a "Briton".

Ireland remained more or less intact from that time on despite many attempts by other people to subdue and control it, including the Vikings and the Normans.

It was during this period that the Scots, Welsh, and Irish each developed their own identities because of the separation, the surrounding environment and external forces and influences. It is thought that the Welsh may be the first true "Britons" although the Picts were obviously there first and were a distinctly different people. Picts were described as a tall, fierce race with red hair.

* * *

This was where the Vikings came in. Until now they had been outside the influence of religion (Christianity in this area) and had a rather interesting philosophy on life in general. The Vikings were large, fearless people who terrified everyone wherever they went. Some historians believe that the reason they seemed so fearless and lived every day as if it was their last was because they were convinced that the end of the world could come at any time. They essentially brawled, raped, pillaged, and lived a pretty "macho" existence. There are probably many men, even today, who admire their lifestyle and bravery. They were not afraid to die because the world was going to end anyway, so why not enjoy yourself? (I suppose in 800 AD this was enjoyment).

It is possible that this was, in fact, their belief, but another possibility is that they may have had beliefs similar to those of the ancient Celts. Celtic warriors literally threw themselves into battle against the Romans because the Celts believed in another world where the soul doesn't die. Essentially it was an *afterlife* and so they were not afraid to die in this world because there was another world waiting.

Regardless, the Vikings had no exposure to the big religions that came out of the Roman Empire; many would settle and eventually adopt Christianity in Ireland and Britain. The Norwegians established many settlements in northern Scotland, and its outer islands, as well as all around Ireland. Dublin is considered to be a Viking settlement. During the initial contact the Vikings looted and plundered Christian monasteries and caused a lot of disruption.

They went on to establish themselves in Iceland and Greenland and it is now generally accepted that they reached as far as Newfoundland, but it was a very small, temporary foothold.

The Danes infiltrated eastern Britain and at one point controlled much of the area held by the Angles and Saxons; their influence can still be found in many areas today.

The Swedes went south into Russia and down the rivers Dvina, Dneiper, and Volga, reaching as far as Constantinople. The Swedes supplied furs and slaves to southern Russia and the Middle East, and were a large influence in the development of the cities of Kiev and Novgorod. They, along with the Slavs and the Finns, developed and controlled this part of the world.

All of this eventually culminated in a short-lived Danish kingdom controlled by Knut the Great (1014-35 AD). Knut even held the throne of England during his lifetime, as well as controlling Norway and part of Sweden, but after his death this Scandinavian empire fell apart. This left Britain in a somewhat vulnerable and confused state and that is usually when someone takes advantage.

*   *   *

In 1066 William (The Conqueror) invaded Britain from Normandy. The small Kingdom of Normandy was never completely controlled by the Franks and the Normans had always maintained ties with Britain. William of Normandy was born around 1027, the illegitimate son of Robert, Duke of Normandy, and was known for most of his life as William the Bastard. Although somewhat average in height and looks, William was quite stocky and proved to be a lot tougher than people gave him credit for. When William was about seven years old his father left for a crusade to the Holy Land, leaving William more or less on his own to evade the assassination attempts of several squabbling barons. Somehow he managed to stay alive and at the age of 20 defeated the usurping barons. By 1065 William had control of a united Normandy.

For some reason William believed that England and its Kingdom was bequeathed to him, probably by his father, and so he took it. He attacked when the Anglo-Saxons were weakened by many years of holding off the Danes, and the Normans quickly assumed control because of the confusion.

The Normans accomplished in Britain what many others had done before them throughout history, which was to be in the right place at the right time and take advantage of chaos and confusion that had built up over many years.

The Normans were then able to quickly establish themselves and control the conquered. William took the land owned by the Anglo-Saxons and gave it to his followers; he centralized power in London where he controlled every aspect of life. He was an extremely brutal dictator and established a system of cronyism and because of bought loyalties he ruled unchallenged. He died in 1087, obese and disliked, and apparently very few people mourned him.

He is considered to be the first "ruling monarch" of the emerging "England" and would be the first of many such cruel dictators that the English would call "King" or "Queen".

While all of this was going on, the eastern half of the Roman Empire, known as Byzantium, remained more or less intact despite a continuous struggle to keep invaders out. Although Byzantium was considered Christian it had several sects, including Catholic and Orthodox who were generally regarded as somehow "impure" by western European Catholics.

Byzantium was now primarily Greek-speaking and Greece itself was reduced to a barbarian-run Slavic state. Byzantium's borders fluctuated continuously as outsiders from all directions pressured its boundaries. A succession of emperors lost and then regained the territory they originally held when the empire collapsed. Despite that, the city of Constantinople was so well fortified that it withstood all sieges and invasions until the Turks finally overran it in 1453.

The western Christians did not help matters any when they came east on their "crusades". In fact, they caused as many problems as they solved. Although their intent was to help hold back the "Muslim hordes", they, themselves, appeared to want Byzantium, as well. From about 1084 to around 1204 when the western Christian forces came in four crusades, the people of Byzantium found themselves trying to hold off the Normans in the west, while still keeping out the Muslims in the east.

During this period the Normans attacked Byzantium several times on their own (apparently not part of the crusades), and so it is somewhat confusing and difficult to understand all the complexities associated with this period.

For several years leading up to the first crusade, the Catholic Church in Rome was at odds with Constantinople and its large following of Orthodox Christians, and so it appears that the crusades had more than one objective. The Catholicism that the westerners brought was apparently different to the Catholicism that existed in Byzantium, and so we have an example of religion integrated with politics and foreign affairs. Rome was exerting its influence.

The Catholic Church had essentially ruled Europe since the collapse of the Roman Empire, because the Germanics had absolutely no concept of structured society. For the last 500 years (500-1000 AD) Rome and the Church had been the central power and even the monarchs of major states bowed to its authority.

When the Frankish Kingdom weakened, control of the eastern half was regained by the Germans. They then began to establish their new kingdom (962-1250), which included Italy and Rome. The influence of Rome and the Church were becoming an undesirable nuisance to the newly emerging German Empire and the Germans attempted to break away from its authority for the first time in history. This was the first real threat to papal authority since the Roman Empire, and during those two centuries there was a bitter struggle between the German monarchs and the papacy for control of Italy. The Pope was still supreme ruler and any threat to his authority threatened all of the west, and so the

Pope and his position and authority was as much about politics and control as it was about guiding God's flock.

During Innocent III's pontificate (1198-1216 AD), he established a papal state in central Italy to protect Rome. England submitted to his will, he was a strong ally of France, and he established the orders of the Franciscans and Dominicans.

The long battle with the German monarchy left the papacy weakened and when the papacy asked for help from France to evict the Germans from Italy, their plan backfired. France was becoming increasingly disgruntled about royalties and sovereignty. Around 1309 France kidnapped the current pope and moved the papacy to Avignon, under direct French supervision. So began the slow decline of the church's authority. The idea of separating church and state began here but it would take another two centuries to accomplish.

As the Germans slowly moved through and past the feudal system and began to form the rudiments of a structured society, they found themselves more independent and leaning less on the church. But the papacy was very reluctant to let go.

The crusades had little or no effect on the Muslims east of Byzantium, but Europeans like to embellish this as part of their history, and talk at great length about it.

* * *

By the start of the second Christian millennium, Europe was slowly beginning to recover from 500 years of total war and barbarianism as the states England, France, and

Germany were starting to settle border disputes and separate themselves politically and geographically.

The economy was still very primitive and based on a landowner-peasant relationship, whereby local nobles or aristocrats literally owned the people who worked for them. The primarily agricultural existence was based on the peasants working whatever cleared or naturally untreed land that was available in the area.

With more stability and less squabbling in many regions, the peasants began to clear portions of the large tracts of forest that still existed in Europe. This allowed them to produce substantially more goods and begin a simple system of fairs and trade. Until then they either did not have the time or means to cut and clear trees, but more likely they never thought of it or even knew how, otherwise they would have done it before then. Regardless, this new discovery helped to establish the big three states and bring more prosperity and stability.

The concept of towns and villages began to emerge and many regions competed for more trade and larger fairs. It's interesting that the Germanics were just discovering this idea when the concept (towns and cities) had existed centuries prior.

Beginning with the new millennium (1000 AD) through the next 300 to 400 years, the feudal monarchies grew in size and power throughout Europe. It was around that time that the Germans were calling themselves the "Holy Roman Empire", but Germany would essentially remain disunited by a series of smaller duchies until the late 1800s when the Kaiser united it.

The Normans and the Franks began what would be centuries of bitter warfare as they attempted to conquer or retake lands. Loyalties of many smaller principalities in France and Germany oscillated between the monarchs depending on how it benefited them.

In England, under Edward I, the Normans tried to conquer and subdue the remaining Celtic holdouts of the Roman Empire. For centuries the English would oppress Scotland, Wales, and Ireland.

* * *

The borders of these developing states, from Western Europe through to China, remained in almost constant motion for many centuries as the Moderns jockeyed and waged war with one another. History books are full of very complete, accurate records of what people occupied which space, who attacked whom, and when it happened, and historians have done a remarkable job to research and record this mountain of information.

However, what is generally lacking in any of these accounts (if you will recall your history lessons in school) is any logical explanation for this behavior.

So, there we were entering the first millennium, and not only were there groups who were very different from each other, in conflict with each other, but now we had groups who were quite similar, or at least quite similar in appearance, in conflict with each other: for example, the English and the French. Both are of Germanic descent, but over the course of several centuries developed or evolved on their own long enough that their societies or at least some of their ideologies became somewhat different.

Even more noticeable is the difference between the English and the Irish, for example, the English being of

Germanic descent (Angles, Saxons, Normans) and the Irish being of Celtic descent. These were two completely different peoples, from different backgrounds, developing their societies or cultures from different perspectives. They evolved with completely different attitudes toward life. Somewhere in the distant past the Germanics and Celts may have been one and the same, but you would have to travel back through evolution thousands or even tens of thousands of years ago to make the link.

What was happening was the groups were splintering at a faster rate than 30,000 years before and it was taking considerably less time for differences to appear. Other influences, such as religion, were coming into play. Each was developing a different version to explain man's existence.

Religion and politics are one and the same in Europe because of the total dependency on the church and its structure.

Europe would continue to struggle for many centuries, and it was not until the 1400s that it showed any noticeable advancement. While Europe continued to struggle to resurrect the Roman Empire, the rest of the world was also evolving.

* * *

In the eastern half of the world, the two other major areas of human concentration, China and India, were going through many of the same growing pains.

China went through a slow process of uniting many smaller provinces into one large empire, while fighting off a succession of invasions from every direction. The Turks were coming from the north, Islamized Arabs were pressing from the west and the large tracts of lands between India and China (mainly Tibet) were in constant turmoil and dispute. The northern border was in constant motion as areas between China and Russia were conquered and then retaken.

Despite all of this China successfully united huge areas under its control or influence and built a very wealthy society based largely on improved agricultural practices. It is still disputed as to whether these provinces were united diplomatically or forcefully, but given the evidence of current archeological finds, the Chinese were also very militaristic. There is no evidence to exclude China or India from the rest of the Moderns and their tendency to accomplish by force what could not be done peacefully.

One thing that historians do seem to agree on is that China was unquestionably far ahead of Europe in economic and social development. For several centuries leading up to the colonial era, China would become the most prosperous and wealthiest society among the Moderns.

Southeast Asia was also developing, mainly under the influence of China, as were Korea and Japan. These areas later developed their own identities and became bitter rivals of China.

During the 1200s and 1300s, two other peoples were about to change the makeup of the world (remember at this point the world as the Moderns knew it was Europe through to China). The Mongols were fast becoming a dominant force. They were excellent horsemen and skilled fighters and under the leadership of the great Khans they made history.

It is now clear that by this point in history the objective was to be the most skilled, bravest warrior in order to gain advantage over the others and combined with the

Roman influence, to establish a state with the conquering people at its head.

I would also like to point out that war was the main preoccupation of the Moderns. Most of this aggressive behavior was initiated or instigated by the leaders and quite often by the extremists of these various groups. Some of the people followed willingly, others only because they had no choice, and this applies to most of the Moderns.

The Mongols and the Turks were the last of the nomadic steppe peoples to terrorize the world. This area had always been very unstable and no one had been able to prevent these nomads from causing mass disruption since the beginning of "civilization".

The Mongols came out of central Asia with total surprise, lightning speed and a military precision that was previously unknown. Their superior horsemanship and tight, well coordinated general staff were too much for the large cumbersome armies to the west.

Most of us are aware that Genghis Khan was the most famous of these people. At one point, he held more territory under his authority than any other human being EVER (more than Alexander or Julius Caesar). And after his death, his successors would continue for some time trying to hold on to all of their possessions. At one point the Mongols invaded Russia and were the only people to do so successfully in winter.

After Genghis died in 1127, his four sons and their generals continued his conquests. His grandson, Batu, directed an invasion at Europe but disputes over leadership stopped him and it is quite likely that the death of the new Khan, Ogede, saved Europe from a similar fate. The eastern Khan, Mongke, had successfully occupied much of China and upon his death and with the death of other Mongol leaders the expansion came to an end.

During their campaigns the Mongols recruited the Turks into their ranks and eventually the Turks outnumbered the Mongols. This conquest would eventually result in the establishment of the Ottoman Empire, made up primarily of Turkish people.

So, everybody wanted to establish an empire, such was the influence of Alexander the Great and the Romans.

History has not treated Genghis kindly and Europeans wrote him into history, as simply being a bloodthirsty moron. One of the main reasons for this was the unacceptability of the thought that a non-European had done what even Julius Caesar could not do. The other was that they were not Christians. This isn't to say that Genghis was a nice guy; he was as brutal as everyone else, but history sometimes has a way of reflecting what we want it to.

The Mongol conquests changed the face of the world from Europe to China. Everyone was affected in some way as numerous peoples were uprooted and dispersed or re-deposited somewhere else. Major parts of Russian, China, India, and what we call the Middle East were reshaped by this massive disruption.

The most significant thing through all of this was the vast dispersion and settlement of the Turkish people after this event. Turkish people and their influence now spread from Europe to China with the most notable effect coming in the Middle East and central and southern Russia.

It was the Mongols who would be indirectly responsible for the Turkish invasion of Byzantium and the subsequent rise of the Ottoman Empire. The Turks essentially just took over Byzantium and the borders remained virtually unchanged.

China and Russia would make it a point to subdue and contain these nomads of the steppes from that time on.

Genghis Khan seems to have inherited the blame for all of the atrocities that occurred during this period. I suppose because he was the central figure, and there is really no evidence to suggest otherwise. However, there is not much in the way of conclusive evidence that he was directly responsible. Let us not forget that the vast majority of his growing army were Turks and it is perhaps they who caused such havoc.

There were, of course, many, many other events happening in and around the main events and sometimes people get sidetracked in all of the details. Much of the time humans tend to stray off onto tangents but we're going to continue to concentrate on the *big picture*.

* * *

All during this time countries, states, and little empires continued to trade with each other because they unknowingly, relied on trade to support their individual societies. This simple trading process would eventually become what is referred to as a modern global economy.

Europe was about to make its move, because Europeans now realized that they lay on and around the Atlantic Ocean, the Mediterranean and the North Sea, and Europeans were about to exploit that. Shipbuilding evolved slowly over hundreds of years and was then at a point where it could become the vehicle for trade. Enter war at sea.

The 1400s and 1500s would see a tremendous increase in world trade, due to shipbuilding. To give you an idea what the world was like 500 years ago, the only European cities with 100,000 people or more were Paris, Milan, Naples, Venice, and Constantinople. Rome, at its peak, had one million.

* * *

People were now totally reliant on farming for their main food source and there would be many periods where people simply did not get enough food, or enough of the right kind of food, and this would directly affect their development.

About the same time, two other peoples were about to change history. The Spanish and the Portuguese were poised on the Atlantic Ocean and because of their location and shipbuilding abilities were set to discover the "New World". They were somewhat isolated from the rest of Europe, both geographically and economically, and so looked beyond the large pond that surrounded them. Spain received some financial backing from Italy, because at this point Venice was the economic capital of Europe (This would later shift to the Netherlands and Germany and later London).

The world was about to change once again. The Spanish, through Venice, financed Columbus, who is credited with discovering North America.

This brings us to a very important point. We are now quite certain that the Vikings were here many years before Columbus, yet it takes many years to fully accept this information and change recorded history, because people, even today, fear change.

Men could experiment with such things as building different (and perhaps better) boats, with their hands hoping to build one that was seaworthy.

History makes it appear as though these newly spawned achievements resulted from conscious effort, but they did not. The necessity for trade spawned the shipbuilding industry. The industry was stimulated by the fact that Europe was surrounded by water and people soon realized that ships were the only way to get where they wanted to go. Trade was something that came about without their even realizing it.

Men were now firmly entrenched as inventors and builders because their *hands* gave them the ability to build a simple model. When the first model showed flaws they could use their hands to build a better one, and this process is primarily the one we still use.

It wasn't long before Europe realized that the present system of trade could not cope with the rapid expansion, especially to the New World. This was perhaps when pirating became the most profitable job in the world. Organized crime has been part of the western free-enterprise system, right from the beginning.

Up to this point, trade had consisted of the simple movement of goods from one point to another by water, because any roads that the Romans had built were unused by Europeans because they didn't know what they were for, and because the economy developed like all of the other facets of society. It was not until conditions became unfavorable that humans were forced to make changes and perhaps those came about because the wealthy trading merchants were losing some of their goods en route to theft by poor starving people.

It is interesting to note that in the 1500s when it was no longer practical to physically move all the goods from place to place and then settle payment, *credit* was established. Transactions were mostly done on paper, and financial powers would get together during the year and settle accounts. Perhaps this was the start of white-collar crime.

At this point the economy was still primarily based on tangible items that were physically moved from place to place. Somewhere along the way the economy began to deviate from this base and wealth could be gained by manipulating intangible commodities, or in other words commodities, which simply did not exist. An economy built essentially on a "house of cards" would be the forerunner of today's economy; for the next 300 years conflicts would remain primarily physical warfare, and then shift to economic warfare.

* * *

Before we get to the great expansion of world trade and exploration there are a few other significant events that should be mentioned.

Rome and the Catholic Church had reached a point of crisis with the Great Schism of 1378-1417, when there were two popes, one in Rome and one in France. France still claimed that Avignon was the new seat of papacy and had support from most of Spain and southern Italy, while the rest of Europe, led by England and Germany continued to support Rome.

The world economy was very shaky and there were several major financial failures resulting in much political unrest during which the allegiance of a region could be easily swayed.

The Swiss Confederation was formed, eventually consisting of eight smaller mountain regions, which managed to break away from German rule by the end of the fourteenth century.

The One Hundred Years' War between England and France, which began around 1337, was the start of a long period of English presence in western France. On the other side, the Burgundians pushed and took control of parts of eastern France, and so the long-standing allegiance between England and Germany began there, as they tried to crush France between them.

England and Scotland were also at war and Edward I was doing his best to take all of Scotland for himself against Wallace and Robert Bruce.

So, the relative peace and prosperity that led up to the 1300s was seemingly lost and Europe was once again in chaos, as England, France, and Germany were back at it.

Life, in general, was pretty wretched unless you were rich. Life for the working poor, or serfs (slaves really) went from bad to worse as regional economic disruption caused many areas tremendous hardship. At that time, life in Europe for the average person was little more than basic survival and was about to go from worse to catastrophic.

In the mid-fourteenth century the Black Death came out of Southeast Asia (apparently) and swept across the known world. The huge financial collapses which were already causing famine and rural upheaval for the working poor, along with the diversion of resources to finance war, were about to have disease, death and mass hysteria added on top. Europe was the last place on Earth anyone wanted to be in the 1300s. If you didn't die from starvation, because the food you did produce was taken, there was a good chance the Black Death would get you.

For Europeans and their descendants the Black Death provided pages of history; what is lacking in these accounts is the main reason why it was so destructive. It is generally accepted that the disease was spread by infected fleas carried by rats and was so potent very few people recovered after contact. However, while that in itself is enough to make it incredibly horrific, it leaves many question unanswered. Why were so many rats running around? Why were rats and fleas so abundant? Why did so many people die from a disease that we don't even think about now?

One of the main reasons why there were so many deaths, particularly in Europe, was because the people were so weak from malnutrition and an impoverished lifestyle. This aspect of life is usually overlooked, mainly because it reflects badly on the people telling the story. Rats were rampant because of the bad living conditions. The recession and famine had weakened people's immune systems. That is not to say that people would not have died if they were healthier, but the severity would have been greatly diminished. In those kinds of conditions any virus or bacteria is a major threat.

This brings us to a very important aspect of human development, the spread of diseases by our little microscopic friends—viruses and bacteria.

Until the Roman Empire, viruses and bacteria posed little threat because they were isolated. The groups of people who existed prior to this had very little contact with one another and many were actually quite healthy partly because of this isolation. They grew closer together in the millennium leading up to the Roman Empire and eventually at some point they produced a "pathway" for the smallest life forms on the planet. Lifestyle and general health also have a lot to do with how ill we may or may not become.

When this new pathway opened up, many diseases, which we now consider to be less serious, such as measles, caused many deaths. This is partly because many groups had not been exposed to such diseases and so had not built immunity to them. In biblical times people were dying for no apparent reason; because of superstition and ignorance these deaths simply mystified people. It was not until quite recently that microscopic life forms were discovered. Humans had no idea why their family member or neighbour became ill and died. Many were persecuted, as it was believed that they had angered the Gods (or The God), and so, not only were they deathly ill, but abandoned as well.

At the point in history when the Black Death ravaged the world, any knowledge that Ancients, such as the Celts, possessed to combat illnesses was effectively destroyed. Any plants that the Celts had been using that possessed immune-building properties were no longer in use and so the Moderns were totally devastated without this kind of knowledge and a lifestyle that could only be described as absolutely deplorable.

***

In the years leading up to the era of the explorer, religious persecution in various regions and corruption in the papacy reached new heights. One of the most notorious, but little talked-about, periods in European history is the Spanish Inquisition. Until the late fifteenth century, Spain was very prosperous compared to the rest of Europe, and there was a major irony in this story, which I hope will become clearer as we progress.

After the collapse of the Roman Empire and the initial invasion of Visigoths and Vandals into Spain, Islamic Arabs invaded from the south (North Africa) and pushed the Germanics north during the confusion. For almost a millennium most of Spain was under Arab control and law, but was essentially multi-ethnic as there were large numbers of Christians and Jews living within this state. This may have been the only time and place in history that all three peoples (Muslims, Jews, and Christians) lived in peace and prosperity (for this long).

The Spanish Arabs, although Islamized, lived very much like the Persians of old, with a tolerant, permissive, and prosperous lifestyle. Christians and Jews were never forced to convert and could openly practice their beliefs with little, if any, interference from the Arabs. The result was a rich and thriving society that the Germanics envied.

It was here, perhaps for the first time that the economy went beyond a simple feudal landowner arrangement, as common people were able to own businesses and property and many non-Arabs held high public office.

It was during this period when the Jewish people first exhibited a seemingly natural talent for business and commerce. Many people in the Jewish quarter of the larger centers were prosperous real estate and business owners and managers, and as the Arabs and Visigoths struggled back and forth for control, each employed many high-ranking Jewish officials and advisors.

This was perhaps the first time since the Roman era that we see anything other than a mono-cultural society. Most societies, until quite recently, were homogeneous, one-race states.

In this unique atmosphere of thirteenth- and fourteenth-century Spain we observe, for maybe the first time, the concept of making money from money. Lending money over a fixed period, with interest to be repaid as agreed, was quite common in this society. So, because everyone was allowed such freedom, cities like Cordoba and Valencia became very prosperous centre of trade and commerce.

Despite having accepted Islam as their official religion, the Arabs of the Spanish Umayyad Caliphate did not appear to have taken it too seriously as they continued to live like Persians.

This was all about to change. Starting in the fourteenth century and continuing through the fifteenth, the Germanic Christians never gave up trying to reclaim Spain, but were generally unsuccessful. In the 1440s a major offensive managed to retake most of the area and the Arabs had to fall back into the southernmost regions. Not wanting to leave their homes, the Christians and Jews stayed and fell under Germanic rule. Over the course of several decades, the new Christian rulers applied oppressive measures to convert Jews to Christianity and the new society became very narrow-minded and intolerant.

Under threat, many Jews converted to Christianity to avoid persecution, or even death, and were referred to as *conversos*. The new monarchy was seriously short of funds in its treasury, the economy was in ruins, and so a campaign to expropriate money and property from those who had prospered began and slowly picked up speed.

An anti-Jewish sentiment slowly built under the new Christian monarchy; paranoia and violence soon set in. Numerous times frenzied mobs marched on the Jewish quarters, killing and looting as they went. The conversos became the primary targets because Christians refused to believe that Jews could convert. As a result, the conversos were closely watched. Many were accused of practicing Judaism in private, especially those who were prosperous and served as bureaucrats and aides to all sides (including during a civil war between two rival kings). Christians of the poorer class showed growing resentment to the wealthier conversos; you might want to remember this point when we get to Nazi Germany later on.

In the late 1400s a local aristocrat, Ferdinand, and a young woman of nobility and English descent, Isabella, were married and became the rulers of Spain, with Isabella being officially in charge as Queen. By this time the Inquisition had officially found status and was backed by the papacy in Rome, and Inquisitors were eager to get started. Isabella and Ferdinand were an ambitious couple who wanted to expand their sphere of influence, but lacked the funds to do it. Isabella was a very young, nave, pious woman who wanted to "cleanse" her country, while Ferdinand was quite devious and power-hungry. The Inquisition provided the perfect tool. Isabella got what she wanted and Ferdinand and the treasury got what they wanted.

Many conversos were brought to trial, usually under false or unfounded charges, and the lucky ones were burned at the stake, while the unlucky ones were tortured and imprisoned, sometimes for years, and then burned at the stake. It is not possible to explain the whole story here, and I am not going to try, but the end result was the death of some, and the expulsion of the rest of the Jewish people from Spain.

After Ferdinand had expropriated all of the wealth and possessions from everyone (one of the bonuses of the

Inquisition), he financed an army large enough to push the Arabs (Moors) out of Spain at last.

In 1492, near the end of the Inquisition, Isabella was also able to help finance an unknown named Christopher Columbus who had convinced her he could find a way to the Far East and bring back even more wealth.

Thanks to the Inquisition, Ferdinand and Isabella were able to play with the big boys, and although Spain had some success during the colonial era, it lacked vision and its narrow-mindedness soon caused its decline. Most of the wealth that the two had acquired was squandered. Because they did not understand the concept of trade and commerce, they never invested any of it, and so it was just a matter of time before Spain would lose its status on the world stage.

Unfortunately, before that happened, something major in human development would take place. In 1492, the Americas were "discovered" and the people there would never recover. When Europeans, in this case the Spaniards, got to the Americas, it was at the height of the Inquisition and Christian paranoia in Europe, and the Ancient societies of the Americas were about to be its beneficiary.

The irony here is that other parts of the world would later become the world centers of trade and commerce, due to a large influx of immigrants, including Jewish people.

* * *

While Europe and the rest of the world struggled with each other, the people in the Americas had, over the past 30,000 years, developed interesting cultures because of their isolation and surrounding environment. In Southern Mexico, the Aztecs had a well-established empire in their own right, while the Mayans had perhaps the most talked-about culture in history located in the Yucatan, and the Incas were a rich and powerful culture which ran down the west coast of South America. As well, the natives of North America had also established themselves with their own unique cultures, which spread to all regions of the continent.

When the Spanish arrived there were apparently about 1,000 different groups of people, each having their own identity, spread across all of North and South America. Although there were obvious regional differences, the various cultures evolved sharing one unique facet of existence—their ability to live in relative harmony and balance with the surrounding environment. This evolutionary trait is primarily what sets the Ancients apart from the Moderns.

Unlike "civilization", there is very little evidence to suggest that the people of the Americas exploited, polluted, or destroyed the natural resources that they depended on *beyond a point that the environment could not rebound from naturally*. That is not to say that they did not have their problems or disputes but, generally speaking, they appear to have existed for centuries in relative peace, with many regions sharing cultural similarities.

Although much of North America was still primarily based on a hunter-gatherer culture, the cultures of the Incas, Aztecs, and Mayans were very intricate and complex with extensive mining and agricultural practices. It is thought that within the boundaries of the Inca culture existed about 20,000 kilometers of road system.

Again, it is quite likely that these people faced some of the same problems that the Moderns had in the other parts of the world, as some are thought to have used concepts such as slavery much like the Moderns. These ancient cultures are just now being completely reviewed and are being seen under a new light as the Moderns are beginning to shed their bias toward indigenous peoples and unravel some of their complexities.

The Incas, Aztecs, and Mayans (and North American natives to a degree) are still a bit of a mystery today, because Europeans almost completely destroyed all of these cultures, and their history now has to be pieced together by modern-day historians and archeologists. They evolved on their own, isolated from the rest of the world, for thousands of years. Over time they developed their own cultures and identities based almost entirely around the environment and so in this aspect alone they were well ahead of the rest of the world.

While people like the Mayans were respecting and integrating with their surrounding environment, Europeans were quickly expanding their exploitation of every resource (including people) because of their totally dependent barbarian ancestry. One of the problems is much of the information that survived the destruction was recorded by Europeans and we have already established their ability (or lack of it) to do it without bias. When one group of people tries to record the culture of another group of people, whom they have never seen before, and cannot understand, the result is a totally one-sided or biased view of that culture. History books are still written this way (although this is slowly changing).

One example of many contradictions is an incident that happened to the Aztecs. In the early 1500s the Spanish had reached the Aztec capital of Tenochtitlan and essentially surrounded, isolated, and starved it into surrendering, no doubt causing thousands of cruel and inhumane deaths. Incidents such as this one and many others for decades of Spanish barbarity are referred to as "diplomacy". From that time on, any brutal acts caused by Europeans around the world would be "diplomacy".

Historians and anthropologists have been struggling for many years to explain the cultures, as they existed upon European arrival and the interaction of the newcomers with the indigenous people. The result has been a completely unbelievable, biased picture because Moderns, even today, do not understand any of the ancient cultures with the depth required to formulate any opinion. We will get into this a little bit more later on.

The fact is, the North and South American people at the time of European arrival were in many ways far ahead of the rest of the world. Many aspects of their culture were unique and if you care to read their history with an open mind, you can easily see these accomplishments.

Here is one possible theory of what happened to the Mayans. When Europeans arrived on Mayan shores dressed in their clunky armor, tights and funny hats, the Mayans laughed at them; that was their first big mistake. Over time the Europeans made it known that they came from a much better, more civilized land, far away and that they were going to give the Mayans this better way of life. The Mayans laughed at them again—their second big mistake. The Europeans noticed a very wealthy culture run by these "heathens" and decided that they would just assume control. The Mayans resisted. Three strikes and you are out. So, the Europeans set about to completely destroy an entire race of people, simply because they did not and could not understand them.

Ignorance breeds fear which breeds prejudice which ultimately breeds aggression.

Picture it in your mind if you would. People coming from a very closed, narrow-minded feudal society governed by the church meeting people who are self-sustaining and don't appear to have a care in the world. Europeans have always mistakenly viewed this as a sign of submissiveness. The fact is, the Europeans didn't expect to find any people in the New World, let alone any that were more advanced. Combine that with a seemingly endless deposit of gold and other precious metals and stones that could be taken back to Spain and even "diplomacy" can be quickly put aside for what can only be described as the complete *rape* of an entire continent.

During the Spanish and Portuguese occupation of the Americas the invaders not only took whatever was at hand, they also established a system of forced labor. The native populations were forced to work their own mines with the gold, silver and other precious metals and stones going back to the Europeans' home country.

In Portuguese-occupied Brazil, the local population was not enough for the amount of resources that could be extracted and so Portugal imported slaves from Africa (Angola) to expand the operation. For about 100 years, Peru was the largest producer of silver in the world, all with free labor. It was a good system, for the Spanish and the Portuguese.

Millions of dollars' worth of gold, silver, and precious stones went back to the homeland; millions more were lost along the way as storms claimed many ships.

One of the most important aspects of what was happening is lost on people of the present day. The people of the Americas, as well as some other parts of the world, had developed their cultures for thousands of years and their entire way of life and the way they *think* revolved around their culture. Once an outside influence disrupted this way of life these people were never the same. What happened in the Americas is a perfect example; once Europeans disrupted a culture and imposed a completely foreign one, they shattered the fragile nature of the existing culture. After Europeans left, the natives' lives were so disrupted that they could not return to their original culture and so had to struggle to understand the new one.

While the people were being raped, not only of their wealth, but also literally, they were also forced to accept Christianity. The renewed fervor caused by the Inquisition had a very destructive effect on tribal culture. People who resisted this new and strange aspect of life found themselves pitted against those who were bribed into following. The result was a divide-and-conquer scenario that was being perfected by Europeans and the Spanish did not hesitate to expand on it.

Religion was one of the tools that Europeans used in their arsenal to occupy and relieve people of their wealth and culture. This also happened to some of the cultures which were founded before the Roman Empire, for example the Celtic people, and it would take only one or two generations to completely alter and destroy a culture. Once the existing cultures were destroyed and their wealth taken back to Europe there wasn't much left. They remain some of the poorest people in the world today, because of this "diplomacy".

One of the most important aspects of the Americas should be kept in mind; much of their culture was very fragile and was based on and around the environment, which is also very fragile. Most indigenous people believed that everything *came from the earth* and *returned back to the earth*. Think about this as we continue.

It is not entirely clear yet how it is that the Ancients of the Americas evolved over that 35,000-year span and integrated so well with their surrounding environment. It has to do with the makeup of the original migrants who ended up there, and the makeup of the environment of the Americas. Somehow, they combined and the result was one of the few areas of the world where human exploitation of the environment and other life forms was very limited.

Their cultures were based on a mutual respect for nature and other creatures. Many indigenous peoples revered other species, such as ravens, eagles, and bears, and retained a great respect for them. The Ancients seemed to recognize intelligence and many other positive attributes in the vast array of wildlife that existed. They developed an awareness that the Moderns did not and realized that the rain that fell and the earth under their feet were directly responsible for their existence, unlike the Moderns, who existed solely from simple farming practices and taking from one another. It is possible that the concept of farming came from watching an ancient culture. The Moderns could not grasp the idea of using the surrounding plants and animals in the same way the Ancients did. Farming was the result and it was the best they could achieve.

Most modern democracies appear to have little concern regarding anything that happens south of the U.S.-Mexico border. They generally consider the peoples of Mexico, Central America, and South America as poor, peasant-ridden developing countries that produce only cheap products and illegal drugs. It is difficult to do more when you have nothing left to work with.

This area of the world (Mexico, Central and South America) is still in turmoil because of colonization. These countries are still controlled by people of Spanish descent, referred to as *Ladinos*, although in the Yucatan and Guatemala, they are the minority as the Mayans still live there and outnumber the Ladinos. Hundreds of thousands of Mayans have been killed by the Spanish, and are still being killed by the Ladinos. The Mayans are referred to as "Indians", and are considered "worthless" by Ladinos who systematically exploit and slaughter them.

All of the land that belongs to the Mayans is now controlled by Ladino dictators who are supported by Western democracies. Any tin pot dictator who promises to embrace democracy is fed millions of dollars by countries like the United States, with very little regard to what happens to the Mayans. The Spanish who went out of their way to make the Mayans dependent on them so they could be more easily controlled and manipulated used this technique consistently throughout the colonial period.

If countries like Guatemala want to become democracies, they have to eliminate as many Mayans as they can; a democracy is majority rule. Quite a dilemma.

* * *

From this point onward the Europeans would consider themselves the centre of the world. Europeans tried to force their way of life on everyone; in some places they were successful, but in most places they were not. The Europeans traveled the entire globe with their wooden boats and developed what was referred to as the Colonial System.

At this point there is no need to go into great detail as most of us are aware of this period. However, what was generally lacking in historical accounts was the destructive nature of this period and the end result of it. If you care to now reread history with a more open mind, I think you will come away with a slightly different perspective.

During the 1500s the rivalry among the various European countries intensified and the Dutch, Spanish, Portuguese, English, French, and Germans all competed to see who could establish the most colonies, thereby gaining the upper hand. So, they all set out and established colonies in every corner of the world.

The world was no longer confined to Europe through to China and, between the 1500s and the Industrial Revolution; Europe would dominate because of the colonial system. It was established around the old Roman system (Europeans are still following Roman laws left behind), the only difference being the people were conquered and assimilated far from the mother country and so each colonial country would have an official representative in the colony to oversee affairs.

Now the sad part about this whole period is that most Europeans seemed to actually believe that they were giving these people a better way of life, and I think it is well known today, that was not always the case.

Under the colonial system, most of the wealth of the conquered country went back to the mother country and in return the people got to live like Europeans. Many people objected to the tyranny over them, because eventually they realized that not only was this new society distasteful to them but they were simply being exploited to produce more wealth for the mother country, and so objected. This period is referred to as *anti-colonial reaction*.

One of the oddities of European thinking is the belief that the colonial system was beneficial to all. Let us think like a European for a moment, using England and the English people as an example.

To the English, colonization was a win-win situation, a perfect society, because not only did they get to take wealth back to England, but the people whom they colonized get to live like them; and why wouldn't anybody want that? The English (at least in their minds) were "helping" the poor naked "heathens" by allowing them to work at a job for more than 14 hours a day. They no longer had to spend 4-5 hours a day hunting and gathering their food. If they worked 14 hours a day they could buy their food—from the English. What a tremendous advantage it was living in "civilization".

Europeans, because of their dependence on trade and evolution through exploitation, could not understand how indigenous people could live without it. When the colonies resisted, the English said, "No, no, you do want to live like us. We're helping you, whether you want us to or not." It was a perfect society, for the English.

During this period the most intense rivalry would emerge between England and France. These two would become very powerful states and bitter enemies and fight each other, not only at home but also in other parts of the world, to see who would dominate.

Many parts of the world would be carved up among the colonial powers and so most of Africa, parts of the Middle East, North and South America, Southeast Asia, the Pacific, the Caribbean, and China were fought over to see who could control and exploit the most wealth, and eventually gain the upper hand.

Historical accounts explained how Europeans opened up the world with gold, cloth, spice, and many other commodities being shipped and traded around the world.

Most are generally aware of the spice trade and how beneficial it was, and most of us learned about this at a relatively young age. These historical accounts did not tell us about the forced labour, slave labour, and millions of people who died as a result of the colonial era.

Historical accounts also forgot to stress how cutthroat the whole era was as each country did its best to either disrupt the others' trade route or take it over by force. The idea was to take as much as you could and this led to war, not only at home, but in the colonies as well. The people of virtually every occupied country experienced the divide-and-conquer concept and were played off one against the other whenever possible.

Prior to the Europeans developing their system of wealth and trade (conquer and take), the rest of the world had been evolving on its own paths, with occasional outside influence. During the Ch'ing Dynasty China had become a very wealthy and self-sustaining culture in that part of the world. History is often very confusing and contradictory and this part is no exception. Europeans go to great lengths to explain how "modernization" and "much-needed change" are necessary in a country that was the most advanced and wealthiest in the world at the time. This leads to the question: If the Chinese were already the most advanced and wealthiest, why would they want to change?

The Chinese were obviously quite different from the Europeans and didn't want to have anything to do with them, mainly because they didn't understand each other.

At first the colonial countries approached China through "diplomatic" channels to convince China that it would be in China's best interest to allow colonialism. Picture this in your mind. People from the most backward part of the world, whose entire existence is based on exploiting people, and is expanding that base, are convinced and are trying to convince others that they, the Chinese, would somehow benefit from allowing a foreign occupation of their country.

By that time it was clear that Europeans had been struggling since the collapse of the Roman Empire, and just could not seem to get the hang of this structured society thing, and so they developed a system whereby they could use and exploit others to their gain. The Chinese, rightly, told them to go away, and that they didn't require their "help".

The Europeans would change that, by force if necessary. So, the various countries sailed over to China and went about invading and establishing colonies primarily on the east coast. The British managed to make their way inland quite a distance and while they played off one part of China against the other, the colonial powers went about removing China's wealth, and China today is but a shadow of its former self. At one point the colonial powers would conquer a part of China, occupy it, and then sell it back. This was all the result of China's refusing European "diplomacy".

***

About the same time another people were making themselves known, as the Russian state began to form in the thirteenth and fourteenth century. The Russians were essentially landlocked and lacked good naval ports, so part of their isolation was geographical and part of it, at times, their own choice. They did apparently try to establish links with the West by sea, but none of their neighbours were overly keen on the idea and so the Russians had to look east and south.

The demand for furs created a push east through Siberia and the Pacific coast was reached around 1640. Initially Russia was an area surrounding Novgorod, which is just north of Moscow. Eventually Moscow and the lands adjacent to it were added in the mid-1400s, and as the Russians pushed east they ousted the Tartars, occupied and controlled all of Siberia, and reasserted control over the remaining Mongol territories in the east.

In the west there was continuous conflict with Poland and Lithuania; these borders have been disputed for the last 500 years. As the Russians moved south they came into conflict with the Turks of the Ottoman Empire and the Caucasus, and so the conflicts that are occurring now began 500 years ago as the people of the Caucasus tried to regain their independence.

The Slavic people followed the European example and colonized everything within their reach, the only difference being that theirs was a land-based expansion rather than sea-based. This attempted expansion by Russia west and south brought it into conflict with the Baltic States, Poland, and eventually, Germany. This area would remain one of the most explosive for the next 500 years, ending only in the Cold War.

In 1613 the first Romanov tsar came to power; this wealthy family would rule Russia until the Revolution in the twentieth century. From this point onward, Russia would go through periods of war and expansion/contraction as it tried to exert its influence wherever it could. The Slavic people, much like the Germanic people, were becoming more reliant on others to help them along.

* * *

In the early 1500s the last of the big religions would emerge out of Europe as a backlash to all-encompassing dominance of Rome, and the Catholic Church. Protestantism was rapidly spreading through Germany and England, as part of their historical alliance and their continuous struggle against France.

First let us look at the word itself. *Protestant.* If you break it up it looks so: Protest...ant. Somehow the pronunciation became blurred and it is now pronounced "Prodestant", but in fact its roots came from protesting the oppression of Rome and so the people were Protest-ants. If you will recall, the idea started back in the late 1200s and early 1300s. Much like Christianity in the Roman times, it grew slowly until it could not be suppressed. Its roots were in Germany where Martin Luther is considered to be the most notable figure to promote the idea, although there were others, such as John Calvin.

The basic premise of this religion was that each individual should be free to interpret Christianity as opposed to one person (the Pope) dictating and controlling every aspect of one's life. Protestants, much like the others, glean from the Bible whatever best suits their slant on life, and add their "Revelations" to the mix. Many Protestant reformists did not hesitate to reinterpret what Jesus Christ said; Protestants today primarily follow the writings of Luther, Calvin, William Orange, Zwingli and others.

Over the next 500 years there would be a huge splinter in the Protestant religion and there are now hundreds of individual sects within the Protestant movement.

Protestantism was the first definitive split between church and state; Henry VIII found it a very useful tool to take control away from the church.

What would follow, over the next 500 years, was a further movement away from religion in state affairs as secularism and humanism regard religion as unnecessary and unwanted in public affairs. The idea of religion in schools and public office is now questioned in Western democracies as these movements maintain that the duties and problems of life should be the primary concern of mankind, and that humans should be responsible and take responsibility for their actions. This came about as Europeans revisited classical Greek society and philosophy, and learned more about power and materialism.

* * *

In America, British colonists tried for years to establish settlements on the eastern seaboard. Spain, having got there first, was content to stay primarily in South America because its extensive river systems allowed for easier access to the interiors and the treasures contained therein. This left North America for the British, French, and Dutch to fight over. The geography of this region was harder to penetrate as the primarily overland route was very labor-intensive, and required the new invaders to be something that they had never been before: self-sufficient and independent. This proved to be an impossible task. How was it then that the 13 colonies came to be? The answer, in history books, is either non-existent or sometimes restricted to a few brief sentences.

When the English first arrived on the east coast of North America, they tried many times to establish some type of permanent settlement. All attempts failed. When the ships returned from England many months later, settlements were deserted, and for years the natives were blamed. For centuries Europeans recorded that their settlers had been murdered by the indigenous savages; however, we know that wasn't the case.

The dependent Germanics of barbarian descent simply lacked the knowledge and ability to deal with this new environment. They inevitably fought amongst themselves and the settlements were self-destructing. After many failed attempts, contact with the native peoples was better established and at some point the natives stepped in and helped the newcomers to survive. They taught the invaders enough about wilderness survival that they eventually got something going. So, it was the indigenous people who were responsible for the whites staying in America, and without their help history would have been quite different. Had the American Indians known how it was going to turn out, they probably would have changed their minds and let the white men starve and kill each other; who could blame them?

By the time the 13 American Colonies came into existence this part of history was overlooked and largely forgotten which is quite ironic when you think about the colonists insistence that the Indians live like them (whites) or be exterminated.

In 1664, the English took control of New Amsterdam from the Dutch and later renamed it New York; by 1733 the colonies were established with an agricultural, commercial, and fishing base. By the 1770s the English had also established an extensive slave trade in Africa and millions of Africans were brought, not only to South America and the Caribbean, but to North America as well.

Until the Declaration of Independence, the colonists were continually at odds with one another because of political and religious differences. There were obvious differences beginning to establish and polarize the North and the South. The North was more commerce-oriented, while the South remained primarily agricultural with extensive slave labor. The mother country (England) was about to inadvertently unite them with a series of oppressive trade laws and taxes. England was in debt from years of war with France, both at home and in the colonies, and since the English considered the colonies simply a money maker for England they tightened their control.

England passed the *Navigation Laws and Acts for Trade*. These laws required that all trade with the colonies had to be carried on ships built in either England or the colonies. The colonies could not export any products to anywhere except England, or another English colony. All European goods had to be bought in England and brought over on English ships. The colonies could not manufacture any goods that could be made in England. All of this benefited England and restricted development in America.

The colonies had been carrying on trade with the French West Indies, selling fish and lumber in exchange for sugar and molasses. The new laws prevented that trade and so the colonies decided to smuggle these products. The English issued search warrants which allowed all premises to be searched from top to bottom.

England then passed the *Stamp Act*, which imposed a direct tax. This Act required the colonies to use stamped paper for newspapers, advertisements and legal documents; stamps cost anywhere from six cents to thirty dollars each.

All of these conditions, which were strictly enforced by the mother country, were considered to be illegal and the idea of the colonies having their own representation in the colonies to deal with such matters quickly materialized. This blatant oppression by England eventually resulted in armed conflict and independence.

For many years after the Declaration of Independence, England tried to blockade and starve the Americans into submission, but eventually had to abandon the colonies. Perhaps the colonists realized how far away they were from the centre of this oppression and that gave them the courage to declare their independence. Even people of the colonial system were having anti-colonial reaction of their own.

The United States of America was still relatively sparsely populated by Europeans and the polarization between North and South reached a peak with the Civil War. The North was opposed politically to the concept of slavery, while the South felt totally dependent on it. This was the primary catalyst for this war. The North was the victor and reunited the states under its control. At this point most of the central and western lands were still populated and controlled by the natives, but as the colonists gained confidence they started to look west.

After the Civil War, the U.S. army was sent west to help defeat the "heathen savages" and bring "civilization" to the rest of the land. Europeans and people of European descent once again set about to destroy an entire race of people simply because they *did not and could not* understand them.

This atrocity by people of British descent was simply due to ignorance and fear.

Ignorance breeds fear, which breeds prejudice, which ultimately breeds aggression.

Americans have quite blatantly documented their history in a very grandiose fashion to explain their struggle against an oppressive England, while totally ignoring what they did to the indigenous people. Interestingly, most of the individuals who would emerge as leaders in these new states were war heroes in the Civil War. Most of the presidents throughout history were military men, a reflection of this society. *People build the society, and the society reflects the people.*

* * *

Back in the mother countries of the colonial powers, the wealthy elite and monarchies were having their own problems. After many years England managed to lure the Scottish Lowlands on side and with them as allies (divide and conquer), it would only be a matter of time before the Highlanders would be defeated. What you are about to read has been included because it played a major role in the development of countries such as Canada, yet many Canadians are totally unaware of this part of history. It also shows how biased records of history can be.

The remaining Celtic people who retreated from the Romans eventually made their way to Ireland (and possibly Britain). While in Ireland the Celtic people adopted Christianity and became some of the most devoted followers of the Roman Catholic Church. As discussed earlier the Scots and the Picts merged to form what would become Scotland.

The culture which developed because of this merger was the Highland clan system, based on the original one (ancient Celtic) destroyed by the Romans. For many centuries the Highlanders lived a primarily self-sustaining life in one of the most rugged areas of the world.

In 1066 the Normans invaded the island and from that point onward attempted to dominate it. History records the Highlanders as being incredibly savage and brutal creatures who fought one another, with clan chiefs who would, in the end, betray their clans. That is not quite the way it happened. The truth is the Normans did not, and could not, understand the Highland culture and so went about their conquering duties with great tenacity. They would first get the Lowlanders on side with promises of land, money, and personal titles and then use the same system as Julius Caesar to separate the clans.

Around 1500 when England followed Germany and adopted Protestantism, the Highlanders remained Catholic. This would only serve to increase aggression and England now had another reason for conquering (and converting) Catholic Highlanders. The Highlanders also continued to speak Gaelic, as they had done for thousands of years. This also amplified the difference between Celtic and Germanic people. The English considered the Highlanders as ignorant heathens, simply because they could not understand the Celtic people.

In 1745, after hundreds of years of trying to stay independent, the Highlanders were defeated and the clan system destroyed, and the *Clearances* began. The English government then passed a law which prohibited the Highlanders from wearing their traditional dress and tartans. At some point the southerners realized the potential of the highlands for grazing sheep, and so, when the Highlanders were finally defeated they were forced to leave their homeland. They were forcibly evicted from their homes and had their homes burned so they could not return. They were then given a choice: go to Canada or Australia, or move farther south to work in the brutal conditions of the mines and emerging factories. They were then left entirely on their own to make their way to the shipping ports with whatever they could carry; entire families, including small children, walked for weeks and slept in the open. The boats carrying the Highlanders to Canada, and the conditions aboard, were described as being worse than the ones which brought African slaves to the New World. Many died from diseases such as smallpox along the way. Many came to Canada; a large number of Canadians today of Scottish ancestry are the direct descendants of Highlanders. History records this as the "Scottish immigration to Canada". It was also recorded that the Lowlanders were the ones who carried out the Clearances, but it was under English direction and when the Lowland policing units could not get the people to move, they were reinforced by English troops. The English then stole and adopted Highland traditions and continued to do so, even after most of the Highlanders were gone, primarily because they didn't have a culture of their own.

Ironically, the Highlanders who went to Australia would help to establish the sheep industry there, and eventually Australia would dominate the sheep and wool market. Apparently there are still some sheep in the Highlands. One of the main reasons that this culture is so badly misrepresented and misinterpreted today is simply because parts of it intentionally got left out of history. The British have never officially admitted to this atrocity, either publicly or historically and continue today to admire and incorporate Highland tradition in their lives.

One of the reasons that the English forced the Highlanders to leave their homeland was because they needed to exploit people who were independent and stout-hearted to settle and develop the rugged wilderness of Canada and Australia. The English certainly could not have done it on their own as they found out in New England, and it was primarily Scots of Highland descent who tamed and settled many parts of what was still a very young Canada, through no choice of their own. The English and the Lowlanders followed along after the hard work was done.

Another event that would inevitably cause centuries of turmoil and many deaths was the settling of Protestants in Northern Ireland. This would be one of Britain's biggest mistakes.

For centuries the English tried to occupy and control Ireland, with limited success. Why they spent about 1,000 years to try to subdue and oppress the Irish is still a bit of a mystery; however, by the seventeenth century they had control of some parts of the island. In the early 1600s the English initiated a movement to settle some of the most aggressive anti-Catholics in Britain, the Orangemen, to the county of Ulster in Northern Ireland. These Orangemen were primarily lowland Scots who had been converted to Protestantism by William of Orange, a Dutch-born reformist.

They were given special treatment and everything they needed to establish themselves, with the intention that they might, in fact, take over, or at least help take control of the island. It was a monumental blunder and caused thousands of deaths over the last 350 years or so.

The result was a tremendous polarization between some of the most devout Catholics on the planet and some of the most devout Protestants on the planet. Ulster would become ultra-loyal to Britain and because of centuries of oppression and resistance the Republic of Ireland would face many of the same barriers as had other anti-British peoples.

The people of the Republic of Ireland today remain the only Celts not assimilated by the Romans or the English.

It is literally the last holdout of the Celtic people after 2,000 years of persecution. Ironically, the people of Northern Ireland have more in common with those of the south than they do with the English, both being of Celtic descent.

* * *

Africa suffered much the same fate as South America; the only difference was that there were many countries involved in colonizing Africa. The British, Dutch, Portuguese, Spanish, French, and even the Germans, the Danish, and Islamic North Africa all struggled to see who could establish themselves and take advantage of sub-Saharan Africa.

The colonization of Africa started in the 1400s as ships from all of these countries sailed around the coast. For the next 400 years the colonial powers were content with establishing coastal ports and relying on bribery and deception to get the black Africans on side. Each power did its best to influence the existing African kingdoms and tribes to deal with them, rather than one of their rivals.

Africa was much like the Americas, in that that the indigenous peoples had splintered into various tribes and occupied most of the continent. There were several well-established respected leaders of these African peoples and at the infancy of colonization, Africa was already a major producer of gold and copper.

Northern Africa had been dominated and controlled by Arabs for centuries. In the 1500s the Turks of the Ottoman Empire invaded and so the Turkish influence was spread throughout the old Arab world, and Old Arabs were fast becoming extinct. The new emerging Islamic states would be far less tolerant and more extremist. Because of their nomadic ancestry, the Turks had difficulty understanding both structured society and their new Islamic faith.

In southern Africa many tribes were played off one against the other in an attempt to win favor with one people so that the Africans themselves would provide slaves from another tribe. This saved a lot of work for Europeans, and so extracting African gold and slaves was the largest trade and wealth supplier, temporarily.

The main reason that Europeans were not penetrating into the interior at this point was the same reason they were having so much trouble in North America. Europeans could not travel very far from their supply line to the home country, because of their dependent barbarian society and they did not possess the ability to be self-sufficient.

The struggle to control Africa reached a peak in the late 1800s. Political partitioning of Africa had been averted until then because of the wild, inaccessible interior, but the Industrial Revolution was about to change that. The 1800s saw a tremendous increase in tension between the powers as first one and then another would conduct a hostile takeover (literally) of another's territory. France controlled fully one-third of the African land mass as most of Northern and Western Africa was under their direct control. Countries like Algeria are still experiencing French interference and most of the conflict and problems that occur today are the result of continued "French interests", but more on this later. The British were on the opposite side of the spectrum, as they invaded and controlled Egypt, much of East Africa and then invaded and took control of South Africa, which had been established by the Dutch. The Dutch eventually managed to oust the British and it is whites of primarily Dutch descent that established the rigid apartheid system.

The rest was more or less up for grabs. Africa would be the only place where Germany was successful at colonization in spite of its geographical isolation and blockade by France and Britain. As the conflicts became more frequent and drew larger attention back home, the Europeans decided to sit down and "carve up" the continent so that the raping of Africa could be carried out without the continuous squabbling.

History books point out that the black Africans were generally "opposed" to this white supremacy on their continent but never really offered any "serious resistance". Historians then go on to explain how Europeans settled disputes with the blacks primarily using rifles and machine guns.

* * *

As time went on many countries who were under colonial control would seek their independence, and any who simply asked the aggressors to leave, would pay the price, and become some of the poorest countries today. So, all of their wealth had been removed and when they finally got their independence, they found that they were excluded from global trade and faced many intentionally placed barriers to suppress any advancement they might try to make on their own. History books go to great lengths to explain this "anti-colonial reaction." They make it clear that in order for this atrocity to stop the invaded countries simply have to "submit" to the aggressors and all will be well.

History books then go on to explain how areas of the world that resisted would be "left behind" because they "refused modernization". Think about this, as you go about your everyday life seeking more independence. The reason they are poor today is because any wealth they had was removed and that is why, and how, the modern western countries became as rich and prosperous as they did, and why the economy is structured as it is. Some of this wealth, of course, would find its way down to the citizens of the rich western democracies such as Canada. The next time you get in your car, or put your boat in the water, or turn on your home entertainment system, perhaps you might think of this.

Europeans built their wealthy modern states primarily from the wealth and resources extracted by colonialism.

* * *

Back on the home front, the "big three" (England, France, and Germany) continued their attempts to best one another and so had many direct conflicts as well as struggling in other parts of the world for colonies. Over time, what developed was more of a one-on-one situation as England and France were both geographically superior to Germany, and deliberately blocked any attempt Germany made to compete in the new Global System being built by sea. This deliberate blockade, in fact, would be one of the primary causes for much of the conflict that occurred among these three countries, yet this aspect of history is generally overlooked. Deliberate oppression of Germany over many centuries would, in many ways, force Germany to look toward expanding a land-based empire, as opposed to a colonial system. The First and Second World Wars were, in part, the result of this struggle and oppression.

This brings us to an important point, the concept of oppression. Oppression was something that developed over time as Europe moved through the post-Roman period. Oppression became a very useful tool for the people who held the most influence and power, and most of the time it occurs without people even realizing it, which makes it all the more dangerous. Not only did entire countries use this tool against other countries, but people used it against their own in the same country, a prime example being the class system that developed in Europe. The rich elite upper-class Europeans oppressed the poorest people in their own country. This was done for a number of reasons and an entire book could be written on this subject alone. However, the short version is that the wealthy elite considered themselves superior humans and needed to maintain superiority (socially, mentally and economically); the common people were considered an expendable resource, to be used any way the elite saw fit. The fact that some humans considered themselves superior to other humans automatically, and sometimes unknowingly, created an oppressive situation. Countries also applied this concept to other countries and other people and many of the world's conflicts were (and are) the direct result of one group of people intentionally oppressing another. This could be done by direct military force or economically through the global economy. The concept of guerrilla warfare and terrorism emerged as a direct result of oppression, but most people fail to see the connection, and so it is the oppressed people who usually appear as "uncivilized" and "the aggressors".

My intent here is not to support one side or the other. I am merely trying to present the side of history that has been neglected.

* * *

So here we are at the Industrial Revolution, but before we get into that, we are going to update human progress. It is pretty obvious that the human race (primarily the Moderns) is totally oblivious to the fact that they are destroying not only their own habitat, but also the habitat of any other creatures that are in their way because of their evolution. Up to this point, destruction has been limited to land, but the Industrial Revolution was about to change that, and expand our destruction to the air and water as well.

Religions such as Protestantism, Catholicism, Islam and Judaism, were now very well established throughout the world, and were also major contributors to centuries of warfare, oppression, and racism. They all struggled to maintain their beliefs and keep theirs from being converted, and to keep their peoples "pure".

Perhaps a budding history student might consider researching as a possible thesis the percentage of history that involved war and humans killing each other compared to the percentage that has been stable and peaceful. History books spend much time explaining the wonderful works of art, and other social enlightenments, that were created through this dark and brutal period. Most scholars tend to gloss over the not-so-wonderful aspects of human development, such as the non-stop warfare, oppression, and perpetual wretchedness of everyday life for the majority of people. Humans tend to give themselves much more credit than they deserve and have become masters of hiding their past aggressions and mistakes. This only encourages it to continue, instead of facing it and dealing with it, because in order to do that all humans would have to consider all other humans as equals.

Something else that is becoming quite evident now, is that as one of the groups of Moderns falls behind the others, they will inevitably use whatever means possible and exploit whatever they have to, to either get ahead or to limit their competition. Inevitably this group will resort to some type of force to take what the others have.

THE INDUSTRIAL REVOLUTION

Throughout the 1700s the colonial powers continued their global expansion and as the wealth from the colonies began to flow in, the gap between rich and poor became more prominent. The poor were still poor, as the treasury continued to grow and the royal courts became increasingly ornate and the aristocracy and wealthy elite seemed to care little about the common people. Europe was about to face drastic change, as it could no longer continue with the primitive feudal system that had been in place for centuries.

In the years leading up to the Industrial Revolution, in which the French Revolution was the most prominent, Europeans slowly advanced their thinking. The beginnings of a structured society, more closely resembling those of Greeks and Romans, began to emerge. This period is referred to as *The Enlightenment*. Most of us growing up can remember *The Enlightenment* from history lessons in school, although I am not sure that most understand its significance. After centuries of struggling to understand and copy the Greek-Roman era, the Germanics of barbarian ancestry were beginning to comprehend what others had done centuries before. This major advancement for these barbarians is eloquently termed *The Enlightenment*, which simply means that they were finally beginning to understand.

The progression of conscious thought (for the Moderns) can actually be followed, starting with the Ancient Greeks and philosophers such as Socrates and Plato right through the Enlightenment, to the present day.

It's interesting to note that many people of the present day consider the human race to be a highly intelligent, advanced species, yet humans were not even capable of recognizing thought until quite recently.

For those people who do not fully comprehend the incredible significance of this, it means that we were neither aware that we were *thinking*, nor understood the simple idea of *thought*.

The Greeks consulted the gods in many aspects of everyday life. The reason that Moderns such as the Greeks worshipped a variety of gods was primarily because they had not evolved far enough to recognize "conscious thought" or to consciously recognize "thought". Nor did they realize that it was they, the Greeks themselves, who were making these decisions and not their gods. It's difficult to say if it was Socrates or Plato who was the first Greek to philosophically break that barrier and spawn the idea of mythology (*mythos*) and rationality (*logos*) as separate. Prior to Socrates, the philosophers of Ionia unknowingly spawned the concept of science with their fascination with and curiosity about the physical world. Individuals such as Thales, Anaximander and Anaximenes were convinced that the world was made up of such elements as water, air, and fire.

From that time onward, science and philosophy would often mix. The most prominent pre-Socratic philosopher was Pythagoras, the inventor of mathematics, who, quite mistakenly, believed "all things are made up of numbers". Many Moderns would then incorporate mathematics and geometry into the area of science. The concept grew from there and would quite often influence Moderns for the next 2,000 years as they tried to define life.

The three most recognized philosophers of modern Western society are Socrates, Plato, and Aristotle. Plato studied under Socrates, and then Aristotle studied under Plato. Socrates was arguably the most controversial and although he does not appear to have had a great deal of influence during his lifetime, his successor, Plato, would change the concept of the modern state.

Socrates was a real boat-rocker and made a lot of high-profile enemies, because he quite often publicly embarrassed politicians who claimed to have superior knowledge. According to Socrates, the political leaders were intellectually unfit for their responsibilities, an opinion which flew in the face of the established concept of Democracy. In other words, Socrates believed that most people could not think on his *higher plane,* and were therefore unsuitable for their positions of authority.

Socrates was quite an odd ball and considered to be eccentric, which makes him either a genius or a rambling fanatic. He refused to recognize or obey any rules set out by the democracy in which he lived. He insisted that only God (or Gods) could be considered truly wise, and that men know nothing. From this perspective, he could be considered a rambling fanatic. However, Socrates is famous (or infamous) for the philosophical concept that what makes him wiser than the others is *he recognizes that he knows nothing.* From this perspective, he is a genius; however, one wonders would an *intelligent* person rant long enough to bring about his own trial and execution? Interesting. In the end, his greatest contribution to modern history is his influence on Plato.

Until then, Greek society had been polarized between Athens and its democracy (ruled by the people), and Sparta, which was purely authoritarian (republic). Plato was the first to incorporate both. Plato was born into a political family, and when Socrates was executed, Plato rebelled against politics and the state, and despised politicians from that time on. This extreme dislike of the rather narrow-minded political leaders led Plato down a new path, one which would change history, but also extract a certain satisfaction or even revenge for Socrates' death.

Plato's goal in life was to design the "perfect society" and his endeavor to do so would transform Greek society to closely resemble the society we live in today.

Essentially Plato incorporated the concept of a republic which was presided over primarily by one individual, with the concept of a democracy which would still recognize each individual citizen. According to Plato, in the existing society the idea of simply achieving freedom is short-sighted, and wastes the talents or potential of the individuals. He insisted that citizens should divide into various groups such as guardians, soldiers, and the common people.

To extract some form of gratification after Socrates' death, Plato established the Academy in 387 BC, designed to educate and train politicians specifically for that purpose. It's unclear how successful his attempts were.

Plato attempted to emphasize the differences between opinion and knowledge: opinion being short-sighted self-interest and desire, and knowledge being on a higher plane or authority. In short, he wanted to ensure that future leaders were above being just ordinary people who simply acted on their desires.

It is Plato who is widely recognized as having laid the foundation of modern democracies. However, the concept of slavery was still accepted and women were still essentially property and these social injustices were also part of that foundation.

It appears that Classical Greek society was in a decline at the time of Plato, and may have influenced his philosophical outlook, but when Aristotle took over from his mentor, Plato, this decline became more obvious.

Unlike Socrates and Plato, Aristotle was not born in Athens, but in another city-state, Thrace, which geographically was closer to Macedonia than was Athens. This geographical distinction expressed itself in Aristotle as a more *logical* approach to existence as opposed to a philosophical one. There appeared to be clearly defined differences among the various city-states, even relating to the way that their citizens thought.

Aristotle moved to Athens to join Plato's Academy in 366 BC and remained there until Plato's death. After leaving the Academy, he ended up in Macedonia as a tutor to a young Alexander (the Great). The Thracians appear to have been more closely related to the Macedonians than the Athenians, socially as well as geographically.

In my opinion, Aristotle did not understand Plato, but simply took Plato's ideas and applied his own brand of logic, which at times came across as somewhat simplistic and narrow-minded. Aristotle's philosophical outlook is very confusing; he tended to categorize every aspect of life in a very logical, rigid fashion. His only contribution to the development of civilization is this logical reasoning which would influence science as time went on.

Further indication of a decline during this period was the recognition of *cynicism* and *skepticism*. Pyrrho insisted that any knowledge acquired to that point (around third century BC), was invalid. People were becoming very uncertain.

It was through the period of Macedonian influence that Greek society became increasingly unstable, allowing the Romans to take advantage of the situation.

Interestingly, there is very little mention of any philosophical advancement during the Roman Empire. It's when a society is in decline that the traditional concepts that have run that society are questioned, and usually it's not until the society re-emerges on the other side of a period of chaos and confusion that the new ideas are incorporated and a new society emerges. However, the new society which should have emerged from the Classical Greeks did not happen, as the Romans rudely interrupted them. It could also be argued that the entire Roman Empire was part of that Dark Age given its brutal authoritarian narrow-mindedness. So, it could be argued that Western civilization went from Classical Greece to the emergence of the modern Western states of the nineteenth and twentieth centuries before the Ancient Greek concepts finally re-emerged, albeit with some influence from the Roman Empire, which may or may not have been beneficial to modern democracy. However this is the path that the Moderns have taken.

During the Roman Empire and continuing until the emergence of the European Enlightenment, there appears to be very little forward thinking in the emerging Europe. Science and social progression were virtually non-existent, as religion dominated society for several centuries. For Europeans, recognizing conscious thought came much later; it was *the Renaissance* led by Italy that slowly began to pull Europe out of the Dark Ages in the 1400s and early 1500s.

Academics in many fields like to acknowledge this period as the new emerging Europe, but in fact, Europe would continue to struggle until the modern Western democracies developed out of the Industrial Revolution. The Renaissance was just the beginning.

It's interesting to note that the new Enlightenment, the religious Reformation, and the beginning of the Colonial Era all happened about the same time.

After centuries of struggling to understand the Greek concepts of philosophy and democracy, the Germanics finally managed to carry on where the Greeks left off. A more progressive way of thinking would slowly lift Europe out of feudalism and eventually create a society that equaled and then surpassed that of the Greeks. In the 1400s, Renaissance leaders like Giovanni pulled out the ancient Greek history books and began to review them, realizing that they might contain something useful.

It was not until well into the sixteenth, seventeenth, and eighteenth centuries that privileged educated individuals like Descartes, Locke, and Kant began to piece together the concepts that Plato had understood. It's difficult to pinpoint which European philosopher was to first recognize "conscious thought" as someone in Classical Greece had centuries before them.

As European (and North American) society progressed through the Industrial Revolution, it incorporated concepts such as *universal education* which would finally allow the Germanics to actually surpass the Ancient Greeks. It was not until education became available to *all citizens* instead of a privileged few that European society would transcend the Ancient Greek society.

During the last five centuries, (1500-2000 AD), Europeans and subsequently most North Americans, would take the concepts of Plato, the Ionians, Pythagoras, as well as a few others, add some Roman domination, and create essentially the society we live in today.

* * *

Feudalism and the monarchies that ran Europe and the colonies were based on what family you were born into, instead of what abilities you had. Despite being poorly educated, the common people recognized an incapable, despotic tyrant when they saw one. Moderns, like the Greeks, Etruscans, Romans, and Persians got things started and created stable societies where people could live and work as long as they obeyed the law established by the overlord. As the numerous groups of nomadic barbarians became more aware of these societies, they wanted desperately to be like them. A few Germanics were allowed into the Roman Empire and were assimilated, but the increasing numbers of Germans, Slavs, and other barbarian groups made it impossible to deal with. The process of a lesser-evolved, aggressive people eventually overrunning a more established group would once again change the course of history.

In the late 1700s and early 1800s, poor oppressed common people in many parts of the world took advantage of a weak economic structure; still part feudal and not yet truly modern.

Despite some government reforms in Britain that led to one of the first elected parliaments, Britain continued its direct occupation and oppression of Ireland, and in 1798 the British Army suppressed a rebellion lead by Wolfe Tone.

The Thirteen Colonies of the Americas declared their independence in 1776. Haitian slaves rose up and rebelled against the French and the Spanish in 1791, and secured their independence in 1825. Rebellions by poor people all over the world created confusion as many parts of Europe, Russia, and South America were affected. All were successful to varying degrees and the mother countries were affected directly because, not only was their *reaction* to oppressive government in the colonies themselves, but even the people of the colonial countries were taking up arms because of their strangulation by the wealthy elite. For centuries the aristocrats from these developing states in Europe used huge sums of wealth and resources to wage war on one another and the poor were totally ignored. The poor spent endless hours toiling on the land and survived on next to nothing.

France was lagging behind in social reforms and was about to get an abrupt reminder. As revolts broke out all through France and Britain, Germany-Prussia took advantage of the situation to invade once more and France found itself in total chaos. Out of this chaos came Napoleon Bonaparte, who rose through the military ranks to become a general at age 28 with what could only be described as a coup. Napoleon became the most powerful man in Europe. Not only did he eliminate the feudal aristocracy and its leader Louis XVI, he seized all lands and property owned by the church and nationalized them. With the backing of several high-ranking politicians Napoleon turned France into a very efficient republic with unlimited military power.

He then set about restoring law and order within France by creating the *Gendarmerie*, a para-military police force drawn from the army. He abruptly turned on the invaders and within a decade had defeated all but Britain itself. Once again France dominated Europe. Its dominance was only temporary, as many areas resented the strict military reign and France was forced to give up the lands it conquered because of resentment and insufficient resources.

Although Napoleon was heavily criticized by historians for being too militaristic in his social reforms and unable to control the areas he conquered, most of Europe would later adopt his reforms. Modern Europe would emerge primarily because of the revolution and Napoleon Bonaparte. The church and the monarchies lost their total dominance and Europe would finally be considered "democratic" officially, although not socially. By 1814 Napoleon had come and gone, and so, after 1400 years, or 14 centuries, Europeans were close to having a society that resembled the Greek-Roman era.

Now that Europe was finally free of the feudal system, a new revolution would begin. The Industrial Revolution would circle the globe and get us to where we are now. However, it was not that easy and there were as many downsides as there were benefits.

Industry began to grow, partly because of the invention of simple machinery, but mainly because of the enormous wealth that the colonies were forced to provide. The steam engine and locomotive allowed Europeans to move more freely throughout places like the African and Indian interiors, leading to even more exploitation of their overseas colonies.

Britain was leading the way, primarily because of Scotland, which had officially joined in 1707. Scotland is one of Europe's biggest producers and exporters of raw materials and most major innovations to get the Industrial Revolution started were by Scots.

* * *

While the Industrial Revolution was slowly getting started, another important event was about to change the history and future of the world—the theory of evolution.

Although Charles Darwin still gets all the credit for this discovery, there were several other people also playing with this idea, some long before Charles was even born.

In nineteenth century England, the scientific community was made up of men only, and most were privileged by birth to be in this exclusive club. That made it very difficult for anyone who didn't meet these criteria. Most of us are familiar with Darwin's historic five-year voyage aboard the *Beagle*, when he acquired specimens and information on many different species. These were all collected and preserved and taken back to England for official cataloguing. Many years later the publication of *The Origin of Species* (1859), would change the scientific world forever. Those who consider Darwin their hero might not want to read this next part.

A French geologist, Benoit de Maillot (1656-1738), is considered to be the first person to write about the idea of microscopic life forms in the ocean being the originators of all life. After that, several scientists had picked up on the idea and it slowly gained prominence. These included Darwin's grandfather, Erasmus, Jean Batiste Lamarck, Etienne Geoffrey Saint Hilaire, Patrick Matthew and Alfred Russell Wallace. The idea sent shock waves through Europe and around the world because it was so controversial. It flew in the face of creationists the world over. Even today religious fundamentalists reject the theory outright.

While on board the *Beagle*, Darwin had an assistant by the name of Covington. Apparently, Darwin and Covington did not get along very well. Darwin was upper class-aristocracy and a gentleman, while Covington was poor, working-class and oppressed. That in itself was enough to cause friction, but everything that Darwin's upper-class upbringing had given or taught him, apparently was bested by Covington. Apparently, it was Covington who was the expert marksman and brought down most of the bird species that were collected. It was Covington who accurately labeled and preserved all of the specimens. While they were on the Galapagos Islands, someone else had to point out to Darwin the difference in the beak shape and size on his now-famous finches.

Back in England, five years later, it was others who identified, classified and catalogued all of the finds that Darwin brought home. Between the previous promoters of the evolutionary idea, and the new information provided by the specimens, the concept of *natural selection* was born. This is where it gets a little confusing.

A brief account of the idea was first published in 1831, before Darwin even left on the *Beagle,* by a Scot named Patrick Matthew, but because Matthew was an unknown, his idea was largely ignored. It wasn't until about 20 years after the *Beagle* voyage that Darwin's *The Origin of Species* was published. At the same time that Darwin was pondering the idea, another man, Alfred Russell Wallace, also a Scot, was a firm believer in the idea and was also working on the idea of natural selection. Based on the information that I have read, it is my opinion that Wallace was the one who expanded Matthew's idea and presented it to Darwin.

So, what exactly did Darwin do to deserve all of this credit? Well, as it turns out, not very much, although anyone who would spend five years on an English sailing ship in the 1800s deserves some credit.

Wallace, it is said, was the "co-founder" of natural selection, but because of Darwin's social standing it got published under Darwin's name. Why did Darwin wait so long to publish this revolutionary idea? Was he waiting for someone else to pull the idea together for him? We may never know. That is not to say that Darwin did not have input in the process or findings, but if you look into his upbringing, he seems to be preoccupied with pleasing his father, and being recognized, but he did not want to be too radical. A very cautious man, Darwin remained reclusive for the rest of his life. It was Thomas Huxley who quite vocally defended Darwin and the whole theory in public while Darwin squirreled himself away in his home in Down south of London. It is said that Darwin was always trying to gauge the response his work was generating. It appears as though Darwin was reluctant to put forward such a bold idea, but it was that or nothing, since being from the upper class he was under intense pressure to be recognized in his lifetime, or be disgraced.

Since then other scientists, not really knowing what to do with this new information followed a very narrow path which led them to intense research focusing on genetics and missing the bigger picture. This was in part due to Darwin's finches and their varying beaks, and the plant experiments that Darwin writes about in his book. These were the catalyst for the genetic research that is happening today. We are going to cover this a little more later on.

* * *

Once the world's economy was centered on the Industrial Revolution, the western countries could mass produce many of their products. Many of the poorer countries developed in ways that did not include machines; understanding and building machines was not something that they had evolved with, or incorporated into, their culture. Our present society here in Canada, like that of other countries, was structured around the Industrial Revolution and now that the Industrial Revolution is obsolete, our society is starting to go through some changes. More on that later.

In Europe, the big three—England, France, and Germany—now had this social development to contend with and the race was on. Europe would become the center of the world because the colonial system had made it the most powerful. The global economy was structured around Europe.

Despite social reforms, the class structure in European society became more clearly defined during this period with the government and upper class still exploiting the poorer people to the limit. In England it was perfectly acceptable to use child labor in some of the most brutal working conditions. It was later abolished, not because of any social or moral outrage, but because deformities were starting to develop that would lessen a worker's worth later in life. It is well documented that children were forced to work 14- or 15-hour days, and quite often didn't get three meals in the course of a day. If they made a mistake they were *strapped*, if they cost the owner anything extra because of that mistake, they were *strapped*, if they even showed any sign of fatigue or loss of concentration, they were *strapped*, in order to keep them alert. This was the hub of "civilization".

During the height of the Industrial Revolution when money and the pride of various countries were at stake, some studies were conducted. In the mid-1800s every aspect of a working class family's life was carefully controlled. The *entrepreneurs* and rich families who ran the industries and factories pretty much had a free hand and there was very little government intervention since governments still did not actually know what their role was. The wealthy would keep track of exactly how much money each person earned and how much each person needed to spend in order to survive, right down to the very last cent in Canadian terms. The idea was that the factory owner could set his wages based on the absolute minimum a family needed to find shelter, eat and buy clothing—the basic requirements for survival. Factory owners would personally keep track of the cost of rent, food and everything else to ensure that nobody had any extra that would be squandered on liquor and debauchery (leisure time).

As factory towns grew, so did the social problems. Each country would boast about how well their workers were treated and lists were prepared of such things as what they ate and how often. Most people subsisted on potatoes and bread, with a little something different here and there when they could afford it. Coffee was plentiful—how wonderful; and so our working relationship (dependence) with coffee begins here. Workers were even provided with lists by their bosses as to what they should buy, much as a current government in Ontario, Canada, did in the 1990s, when they provided a list of what people on social assistance should buy and what they could survive on. Even their living quarters were scrutinized for size and wall thickness to ensure that their workers would have just enough privacy and enough room so as not to go insane because that was a loss to the wealthy.

The working-class people of Europe in the 1800s had *far less* than humans 10,000 years ago. This was the society that Europeans were forcing on others. Studies were also conducted to understand why some people spent every bit of money they earned, while others actually managed to save a little. This was puzzling and disturbing. Entrepreneurs and society strongly recommended that those who could not save anything should follow the example of those who could.

Each European country's government and rich elite did their best to ensure that their working class was better than someone else's while still squeezing the life out of them. A basic concept developed: the controlling body would allow the common people just enough to provide for themselves and if they showed any signs of getting too far ahead the government or rich elite would essentially appropriate it somehow. In today's terms, taxes are raised, and today's system is basically the same because the more money one makes the more tax one pays. This system developed as a direct result of the Industrial Revolution, and is still designed to make it very difficult to get ahead.

This was simply to ensure a permanent work force that could provide an uninterrupted flow of production. If people got far enough ahead that they did not have to work six or seven days a week, then production would be disrupted. The system was designed to exploit people as well as resources, and once the concept of social consumerism was spawned the demand always exceeded the supply. The objective, then, was to constantly feed that demand. Demand has now matched supply, but more on that later.

It was during the Industrial Revolution that invention and machine-making to increase productivity and profit made their debut. The revolution was centered on these new machines which upset many working people. Some went on machine-bashing excursions because the machines were taking the place of people. It appeared the quest for productivity and profit was more important than human life. This may sound overdramatic, but if society is structured so that one *must* have a job to survive, then not having a job is threatening one's very survival. Is it not?

History books go to great lengths to explain how this new revolution "modernized" society, improved life, and expanded "globalization". However, if you read books which contain the actual writings of everyday people who lived during this period, they portray a much different perspective. Life in general was not rosy. Factory and mine conditions were incredibly brutal and it was mainly oppression and deliberate exploitation that forced people to accept factory life. This is called *conditioning*. Interestingly, the average person's lifestyle remained virtually unchanged for the next 200 years. Perhaps the history books are referring to the already wealthy upper class, when they talk of advancements. If the revolution was expanding the global economy by starting up new mines and factories, expanding old mines and factories, and building railways to move all of these goods, commodities and materials, yet the average person's life remained virtually unchanged for decades, then exactly who was the revolution benefiting?

The Industrial Revolution also spawned some of the worst exploitation of the environment and expanded pollution to every habitat in existence (land, sea and air). It was allowed to happen because the Moderns had absolutely no idea what they were doing. It wasn't until the 1960s that the Moderns began to realize the mistakes that they had made. Pollution was by then a very visible problem. In effect, the Industrial Revolution would be the crowning achievement of exploitation by the Moderns. In an attempt to justify the mistakes and pollution, many people will try to argue that the reason we live such a good lifestyle today is because of this revolution. But this is incorrect. This better lifestyle was the result of the common people's increased pressure on government for better working conditions and social programs. In Canada most of this occurred after the First World War when Canadians gained more control to govern ourselves and moved farther out from under direct British control and the oppression that went with it. It is only as we start the third millennium that some newer history books are beginning to include at least some of the atrocities and mistakes that the Moderns have made.

The Industrial Revolution resulted in a dramatic increase in urbanization as more and more people from the countryside moved to the larger centers. The monstrous cities that exist today were spawned by this revolution. As the cities grew, so did the social problems because people were losing touch with the outside world around them. Many were born, lived and died in these sprawling, drab, concrete lands that oozed boredom and fostered total dependence on their municipalities.

This new revolution was moving goods and raw materials much faster and creating a system of trade that grew more complex every year. Customs and tariffs were established and the "big three" (Britain, France, and Germany) were now at odds economically, as well as physically and socially.

After gunpowder was invented in China, a few centuries earlier, the Europeans (not surprisingly) were the first to develop it solely for warfare and killing. The arms industry was underway, led by Krupp in Germany, and it appears that building bigger guns for Moderns to kill others, including other Moderns was a major contributor to the Industrial Revolution.

The first part of the revolution which primarily involved coal and iron production quickly transformed into a second phase with the development and expanded use of steel and electricity. With the advent of the steam and then diesel and electric engines, the Industrial Revolution was unstoppable. Britain, Germany, and now the United States primarily led the way as new industries developed at a phenomenal rate. The newly expanding chemical industry, that was primarily coal by-products, spawned many other industries and products, all of which dramatically increased our destruction of the environment.

The poor were still poor, but slowly began to organize themselves. Labor unions began to form in the nineteenth century. Europeans and North Americans who were inspired by this new society to expand business, commerce and trade were still doing it at the expense of the common people.

Although these newly industrialized states had modern elected governments, they were still in their infancy. Government, even at this point, had little control over how industry conducted its affairs. The idea of separation of church and state began about 800 years before this revolution; with England and Germany making it official in the early 1500s. Yet, until very recently, governments still had very little power and did very little in the way of social reform. The main reason is Europeans do not understand the concept yet and even as we start the 21st century the Moderns are still struggling to understand what makes a fair and just society.

In 1871, Kaiser Wilhelm I united the various Germanic provinces into one country, Germany. In Europe, the various splinter groups were running out of room and there was a mad dash leading up to the First World War, to grab as much land as possible. What happened next is referred to as *nationalization*, which means that with nowhere else to go, groups of people begin to draw borders around themselves. However, these borders were not yet fixed or permanent, as the First and Second World Wars would change them again.

Back in the Middle East, the Ottoman Empire (Turkish peoples) was still trying its best to expand, and would later fragment into the Middle East countries that we know today: Iran, Iraq, Arabia, Syria, and the rest. Many of these countries would develop very rigid religious regimes, partly because of their nomadic ancestry, their difficulty understanding structured society and their religion (Islam), and partly because of Western interference in their affairs because of the increasing need for oil.

In the years leading up to the First World War, European countries were still struggling with one another for any unclaimed territory. In case you haven't picked up on it yet, the human race started to kill one another hundreds of thousands of years ago and still is. Aggression and war have been major parts of our evolution.

At that point, Bosnia was under Austro-Hungarian rule. The Hungarians somehow managed to gain equal status with Austria as the result of an Austrian-Prussian war. The apparent fuse that started the First World War was a struggle over Bosnia by Serbia and the Austria-Hungary alliance. The new wave of nationalism sweeping Europe was creating increasing tension, as each state tried to expand its borders as far as possible before they were officially drawn. This set in motion a series of rivalries and alliances that changed partners faster than one could keep track. The reasons for the multitude of changes are very confusing and complicated and may never be fully understood, so I am not going to bore you with the details. However, I will list here how it played out.

In 1879, Britain and Austria-Hungary were allies. Germany and Russia were allies. France was independent, as were Spain, Italy, and Turkey.

By 1883, Germany, Austria-Hungary, Russia, and most of the Balkans were allies. All others were independent or neutral.

In 1887, Britain, Austria-Hungary (again), Spain, Italy, and most of the Balkans were allies. France was still independent but gaining some Russian support. Germany and Russia were allied.

In 1891, Britain, Austria-Hungary, and now Germany, Spain, Italy, and most of the Balkans were allies. France and Russia were allied.

In 1897, the whole thing fell apart. Britain was independent, France was independent, Germany and Italy were allies, and the rest were confused.

In 1904, Britain and France were allies and the rest were still talking.

In 1909, Britain, France, Russia, and part of the Balkans were allies. Germany, Austria-Hungary, and Italy were drawing closer together.

In 1914 at the outbreak of war, Britain, France, Russia, Italy, and Greece opposed Germany-Prussia, Austria-Hungary, Bulgaria, and Turkey. Poland and Lithuania became pawns between Germany and Russia; this would not be the last time they would fight over them.

Germany then tried to conquer France as quickly as possible, but could not and so faced a war on two fronts, one that it could not win. A 400-mile line was drawn and a stalemate quickly developed, eventually causing hundreds of thousands of deaths.

In 1917, German U-boats sinking American ships drew the United States into the war and the addition of one more country managed to end the war.

The First World War produced another major industry, the development of military hardware and armaments strictly for warfare. This achievement allowed Moderns to kill each other on scales previously unheard of and much more efficiently. Armies began to distance themselves from their enemies and the objective became killing the enemy with a minimum of casualties to your side.

Very impressive. Very civilized. This new innovation would eventually lead the Moderns to refer to war as "civilized engagement".

The Industrial Revolution spawned chemical and biological weapons of war. Poison gas was used for the first time in history as a weapon to kill, and although biological weapons did not receive any attention yet, they could not be far behind. Interestingly, the world's worst flu epidemic occurred right about the time these combatants were experimenting with biological warfare. The Spanish Flu, which apparently originated in the U.S., killed an estimated 50 million people worldwide. Oddly, the flu primarily attacked healthy men between 20 and 40 years old; the age of soldiers during the war. Coincidence? We'll see.

Despite studying this part of history with an intense interest, I failed to find any *logical* reason for the "Great War". Until then warfare between Moderns had remained virtually unchanged since classical Greece. Opponents on both sides amassed as many capable men as possible and opposed each other on the battlefield. They then advanced toward each other with the objective of breaking the other's rank. Long-range guns were about to take Moderns down a new path.

In 1917 another major event would reshape the world. After many months of war and poverty and no end in sight, Bolsheviks, a class of poor, working Russians, banded together and overthrew the oppressive Tsarist government in Russia. The result can only be described as absolute chaos that lasted until about 1929 when Stalin seized authority and became the first Communist dictator of the new Soviet Republic.

The Tsar as an ally was overthrown, and Trotsky was inciting the revolution to spread to Europe, for some reason thinking that what they had started was a really good thing. This disruption in the East may have actually helped to end the First World War.

Almost immediately after the revolution, "White Russians" attacked the Bolsheviks, with the help of foreign powers and a three-tier civil war ensued. The Bolsheviks managed to hold on and after the opponents withdrew, strikes and riots broke out and military mutiny was commonplace. The new regime under the Communist Party quickly and ruthlessly suppressed any dissenters. The economy was in ruins and Stalin forced outlying areas to send food to the urban centers. The Russian people had just replaced one oppressive regime with another.

* * *

During all of this, China was still desperately trying to keep out the European colonial powers, as well as Russia and Japan. The British were well established as the most aggressive and relentless people on the planet and since 1793 had continued to invade and disrupt the country. After having colonized India, Britain tried to occupy China from both sides. China had successfully suppressed a growing opium trade for decades until the British defeated the Chinese forces in the mid-1800s. The British then expanded the opium trade as another exploitable resource. As a result China was finally forced to allow foreign invaders to occupy various ports. France was pushing north from Indo-China (Laos) and Russia was pushing south. The Japanese were doing their best to take what they could and even the Germans were trying to establish a port in the northeast. China became a major target to "conquer-and-take" societies emerging through the colonial period.

The period from the mid-1800s until around 1912 saw China literally disintegrate because of outside aggression. Millions of Chinese died over a period of two centuries because of their refusal to "modernize" and be "European". Eventually, after so much intense pressure from outsiders, parts of the eastern seaboard were colonized and Europeanized for a short time. European reforms and industrialization began to appear and work their way inward, and China was forced to give Hong Kong to Britain. The Japanese then launched a major offensive from the north-east around the turn of the twentieth century and eventually occupied most of the eastern seaboard until the peasant-based Communist party forced Japan out after the Second World War.

***

Many mistakes have been made and are still being made, and it is very difficult to admit one's mistakes.

* * *

In the late 1800s the United States had plans to occupy not only Canada, but also Central America, South America and the Caribbean. It purchased Alaska from Russia as a means to box in Canada and eventually control it. The Confederation of Canada in 1867 was the one single act that prevented it, as the United States had plans to incorporate most of the western provinces.

Ironically, the one country that so proudly boasts of its freedom and independence (U.S.) was now joining the colonizing countries for control of the world and its people. The U.S. set about annexing or occupying by force, Hawaii, the Philippines, and most of the other Pacific islands. It then turned its attention south and declared war on Spain for Mexico, although the Spanish were quickly losing control of their properties anyway.

The United States, as early as 1823 with the Munroe Doctrine, treated all of Latin America as part of the U.S. There were several attempts to take Mexico but they all failed; however, the U.S. did have some success in parts of Central America, South America, and the Caribbean, taking Nicaragua in 1909, Panama in 1903, Puerto Rico in 1898, Cuba in 1903, and Venezuela in 1895. In short, the U.S. had plans to occupy and control as much of the world as possible. This still appears to be one of their primary foreign policies but more on that later.

The U.S. then set its sights on China—why not? Everyone else had—because China still had potential for controlling and extracting great wealth. Prior to the 1949 Communist Revolution in China, the U.S. was actively engaged in financing the Nationalist Party which was fighting a civil war with the Communists.

The focus of the Western powers was now shifting. Up to this point the objective had been to take by force any wealth and to turn the locals into forced labor to exploit whatever was still exploitable. As the global economy began to take shape, because of the Industrial Revolution, the focus shifted to controlling foreign markets through aggressive capitalism and the economy. Aggressive capitalism was the primary motivator for anti-communist movements. Communist nations did not want to allow aggressive capitalist countries to take advantage of their country.

* * *

Although secret societies are not as important or have as much influence as they once did, I want to include them because they still exist and are still evolving and as JFK once said (I'm paraphrasing); there is no room in a tolerant modern democracy for these types of organizations. (This little section was revised in 2006).

In 1865, a secret society was founded in the U.S. called the Ku Klux Klan. This organization was a backlash to the increasing number of immigrants and black slaves. The U.S. civil war was based on slavery and the right to own slaves. Once the North set about freeing black Americans after the war, the KKK was born. Membership requirements were quite simple: you had to be white and a "native-born" American.

Long before the KKK was born, another secret society, originating in Europe, was already fairly well established. The Freemasons began as a workers' guild in

Europe. During the Middle Ages stonemasons were highly respected and sought after for constructing churches, towers and other buildings for the aristocracy. Freemasonry today has very little to do with building with stone and more to do with recruiting people who share similar ideologies. Their fundamental beliefs are still a mystery and I personally have talked to some who will admit that they 'don't get it'. They have some kind of link to the pyramids, the shiners as well as 'space beings', (whatever they are). I highly recommend searching secret societies on the internet (Wikipedia) as I don't want to get onto any tangents for too long. A former Mason has put his initiation ritual on the internet (one of the highest degrees they bestow), and if anyone who reads it actually understands it you're doing better than I am.

Many American colonists were members of the Freemasons, including George Washington, as were many other high ranking leaders of the American Independence movement. As the Middle Ages were replaced by the more modern states, the Freemason society dwindled and over many years its membership and interest in it was all but defunct. Someone decided, several decades later (probably in the United States), to rebuild and renew interest in the Masons as Europe moved into the Industrial Revolution. The original meaning and purpose had long since vanished and so the new members did their best to continue the old traditions and secret initiations. The society was broadened to accept anyone who met the criteria, which was, primarily a white-is-right attitude that originated out of Britain.

It's thought many KKK members were Mason rejects mainly because they were too unstable and prone to violence. The Masons preferred a much lower profile. These groups reached their peak of power in the 1920s as many presidents, senators, governors, mayors and high-ranking police officials were members of one or the other. Eventually it became politically incorrect to be publicly associated with these groups and they lost most of their influence over the next 70 years or so. The KKK had limited success in Canada mainly in the western provinces. Although the KKK and Masons still exist today their numbers have steadily declined and many citizens in towns or larger urban areas are not even aware of their presence.

In his book *Hooded Americanism,* David Chalmers claims that Rome and the Catholic Church had been the main enemy of these groups, although, Blacks, Jews and all other persons with dark skin were also targets for their Protestant-based white hatred. I can't verify that, but I do no know of any white Catholics who were lynched or shot.

The Masons today publish literature that says they accept any person regardless of ethnic background, but I am not sure why someone of African or Asian descent would want to join what has always been a white boys' club.

The KKK openly threatened Blacks to keep them from voting, and at one point President Grant had to send U.S. troops south to protect the new citizens. By the end of the First World War the United States was considered to be the new World Power, and had inherited the title as the most aggressive country and people in the world.

Secret societies were primarily developed do to ignorance. I think you will find that the majority of people who join these groups are just people who lack knowledge or understanding about other peoples and their cultures or societies. There is one exception.

There is one other that should be mentioned that has formed quite recently. In 1954 the Bilderberg group was formed and although they are not a typical 'secret society', their agenda and activities are, well, secret. . It consists of over one hundred very rich and/or powerful people who meet secretly every year to discuss global events. Again, I recommend the internet were you can find hours of very interesting reading on this group. I'm not going to get into great detail here as I'm still researching why they exist and what they think their function is, however, there are some interesting connections with their meetings and world leaders who get elected.

* * *

In the years between the First and Second World Wars, European countries were in disarray politically and economically. This instability caused a major change around the world. Most of the countries still under colonial control took advantage of Europe's weakness to initiate their own independence, and to free themselves from decades of white supremacy and oppression. However, all that they could accomplish at that time was to establish their own nationalities, under forced colonial control. The Middle East would establish independent nations from the breakup of the Ottoman Empire, but their greatest resource (oil) was still controlled by Britain and France. This was a powerful reason for maintaining dominance and resisting independence.

During the instability, many new political groups formed as people began to see daylight for the first time. The Chinese were still struggling to keep Russia and Japan from occupying and exploiting various parts of their country. Many smaller splinter groups had materialized throughout the development of Europe and considered themselves as a separate people. They included the Kurds, Gypsies and

Palestinians, just to name some, but most were ignored, oppressed, or persecuted by larger more aggressive regimes.

Europe was in ruins after the first Great War, as all the major players were suffering major economic strains having spent all their money fighting one another. Unemployment and inflation were running wild and new political parties emerged. After the Central Powers collapsed most of Eastern Europe was restructured, as the newly independent states of Finland, Estonia, Latvia, Lithuania, Poland, Czechoslovakia, Romania, and Yugoslavia were born.

In an attempt to save themselves, Britain and France formed the League of Nations, which Germany eventually joined in 1926. It was a feeble attempt to bring stability back to the world after the big three had met in their biggest struggle to date to see who the master race was. Much of the resources that had been forcibly removed from the colonies had been spent on the big fight, and they were desperate to get back to exploitation to rebuild. The only problem was that the "big three" were no longer the biggest. This conflict was global in nature and someone forgot to inform them that the rest of the world was just as big. The U.S., Russia, Italy, and Japan were now major players who ignored Europe.

The League of Nations actually set out proposals for disarmament, but nobody was listening. Europe was no longer the big player in the world, and the U.S. and Japan were just getting started. The period between the World Wars was very unstable and there was never any hope for peace. New and old alliances were explored and borders were still being disputed. Since the collapse of the Roman Empire, the Germanics and their descendants and the Slavs and their descendants would be the most aggressive people on the planet. Their attempts to re-create the Roman Empire and build a stable society would take centuries and cost millions of lives, and they are not finished yet.

The new global economy created by the Industrial Revolution was advancing at an incredible rate. These Moderns had never seen an economy or a society like this and so it was very unstable and subject to frequent collapse. Starting in the early 1800s there was serious economic disaster on a regular basis, about every 10 to 14 years. This was especially noticeable in the U.S. as the western expansion took off. Massive land buying and speculation primarily for railroad building always led to imbalances as people rushed to acquire land that they thought was in the path of the railroads and productivity far exceeded demand throughout the industrialized world. The result was economic collapse on a regular cycle, which finally ended with the crash of 1929 and the Great Depression.

***

Still between the big wars, there were other smaller wars and conflicts in Europe and around the world. Have I said this before? I hate to repeat myself, but it seems as though the phrase "Europe was in chaos and confusion" has been the most common for the last 1500 years. Please, somebody stop me when we get to the "civilized" part.

Most civil wars are treated by politicians and historians as just that; one side fighting another within the same country. Sometimes that is the case, but usually there is more to it. Such was the case with the Spanish Civil War. History records that the existing government was a democracy and included the military, the political right and the Roman Catholic Church. On the other side were the republicans, anti-clericals, anarchists, socialists, Communists and autonomists (Basques).

In many cases these domestic matters could probably have been solved more quickly and more peacefully if left to the people involved. What usually escalated the conflict and caused more death and destruction was outside influences backing one side or the other. Some outsider somewhere will have "interests" and so will back whichever side best serves their "interests". This has been the case throughout history and this dynamic is still being played out all around the world today.

In the case of Spain, it leads to the question: why would people rise up, or take up arms, to overthrow a government which was considered to be fair and tolerant? Interesting. There is one very interesting dynamic that is still occurring today that started many years ago. Throughout the nineteenth century and the beginning of the twentieth and going back throughout European history, the common people have consistently revolted against their governments. This was primarily due to oppression, extremely bad living conditions, and poverty. Throughout European history the wealthy aristocracy lived in plush palaces with a lot of pomp and ceremony while the common people generally lived in squalor. The rise of Communism, Fascism, and Nazism was the direct result of oppression. The common people for the first time formed political movements and assumed control during periods of instability. That is not to say that these systems were better, but their rise was inevitable.

In the case of China, the common people needed an equally aggressive system to keep just about every country in the world from taking it over. The reason China is a Communist regime today, is not that the Chinese people are more evil; it is because of centuries of primarily western countries trying to rape it. We have a tendency to be very short-sighted.

As a result of primarily ignoring the people and having as many human rights violations at home as abroad, people like Stalin, Mussolini, and Hitler were swept to power. The irony is that they would turn out to be more oppressive and dangerous than the old regime. Once again the sides were forming up for another big fight, except Communist Russia was now a wild card. Both sides tried to neutralize Russia to keep it from becoming involved.

In 1936 Germany, Italy, and Japan formed the Anti-Comintern Pact (Axis allies). After Hitler was swept to power in 1937, the Nazis did everything they could to reverse or ignore any pact or treaty coming out of the First World War. Hitler then systematically destroyed all other opposition in Germany and became a dictator. Germany was pulled out of the Depression primarily by a mass buildup of arms which stimulated industry.

So, Communists, Fascists, and Nazis rose to power and they became the majority. If you were not with them, you were against them. To a large degree this phenomenon was economically and socially driven, but for the Nazis there was also a strong nationalist element (racism). Since the breakup of the Roman Empire, the Jewish people had been dispersed throughout the world, and this now included the New World (Americas), as well as the Old World (Europe). Earlier, it was mentioned about how the Jewish people had a "knack" for business in medieval Spain, and how their society generally prospered compared to many others. The same story was playing out throughout Europe and North America; the Jewish people, regardless of where they were, usually prospered because of this ability and in fact played a large part in the development of today's global economy.

The only problem was that the Jewish people concentrated themselves in isolated enclaves within a society, to stick together because of their faith. This isolation and prosperity caused a lot of resentment in the societies where the Jews were very prominent. In a tolerant democracy they were generally a benefit; in a narrow-minded authoritarian Aryan dictatorship they were considered a cancer. What happened in Spain in the 1400s was about to be repeated in Germany in the 1900s.

The resentment against Jewish people was not limited to Nazi Germany, as anti-Semitism was on the rise everywhere in the modern world. The Ku Klux Klan, perhaps as no surprise to anyone, openly supported and endorsed the Nazi party and the persecution of Jews. Even high-profile celebrated citizens like Henry Ford of the U.S. were open supporters of the Nazi party. Ford was photographed in the 1930s personally accepting a "high achievement award" from Adolph Hitler. Until the United States entered the war, the North American auto industry (Ford and General Motors) sold whatever they could to the Nazis, and supplied many vehicles and parts.

All of the white majority countries, including Britain and France, had groups that supported anti-Semitism, and Rome and the Catholic Church were oddly silent on the matter. Perhaps Hitler saw this global dissension as a green light to take care of this "problem".

Let's return to the upcoming war. In 1936, Germany regained control of all lands it considered theirs (and had been theirs) until the First World War, when the British and French controlled areas like the Rhine in an attempt to control Germany. In the same year, Italy began to flex its new muscles and greatly strained any diplomatic relations it had with Britain and France. In 1937 Japan launched a full-scale invasion of northern and central China. Japan had been adopting (and liking) for years this Western concept "take by force" what can't be accomplished peacefully. In 1938 the crisis was coming to a head as Germany annexed Austria, taking it over whether the Austrians wanted them to or not.

As the European countries had entered into the colonial era, and set out around the world looking for wealth to bring back to the mother country, Russia and Germany were blocked in. They had very few good naval ports and they were poorly situated with France and England blockading (using naval power) their attempts to get out to the Atlantic Ocean. As a result, Russia was not even a colonial player and Germany's colonization was very limited, and so these countries looked *inward* to expand their power and to keep pace. So, ironically it was England and France who were perhaps as much responsible for the great wars as anyone.

By then it was apparent that the Nazis had to be taken seriously, so Britain and France initiated diplomatic talks with Hitler to see if they could control him. The historic meetings between Chamberlain, representing the West, and Hitler and his senior staff have been immortalized on film reel and are still talked about today. The only thing missing is what was actually said in those meetings because there are some events that occurred that just don't mesh with what we were told.

People who were not privy to the high-level discussions rationalized Hitler's ambitions and allowed him to take over Austria and then half of Czechoslovakia in an attempt to appease him and keep peace in Europe. This came from a country (England) that would go to war at the drop of a hat. These events and many that followed have yet to be rationally explained. First, Britain allowed Germany to take over any territory that had German-speaking peoples. Had Britain's allegiance shifted again, from France back to Germany as it had been throughout the history of Europe? Or, were they just desperately trying to avoid another conflict because they (England) were broke?

Germany continued to slowly expand on the mainland with little opposition. Prior to the outbreak of war in 1939, Britain was helping France to occupy and strengthen the Maginot Line, which was a heavily fortified border between France and Germany. They were also the primary opposing force in Belgium and Holland. In 1939, Germany rolled over Poland with little resistance. France had to know that it was next, but because of some "confusion" between British and French troops the Germans quite easily broke the Maginot Line and pushed into France despite the fact that it (the Maginot Line) should have been almost impregnable. Britain reasoned the most likely place for a major German offensive would be through Belgium, and guess what? It was; how odd. France was overrun and occupied with minimal effort. There were many other unique events that happened during the first half of the war that have yet to be explained because they contradict the standard rationale and explanations.

The first was Dunkirk. Why did Hitler push the British troops to the best evacuation point in France and then suddenly stop? Was Hitler a kind, compassionate man? Or, had this been prearranged? Until 1941 when "outsiders" entered the war, Germany pretty much did whatever it wanted.

The question is did Britain *allow* it to happen, having entered into some kind of an agreement with Hitler? Hitler obviously had read history because many of his ambitions closely paralleled the Roman Empire and the British Empire.

It was obvious that Hitler greatly admired the English and was aware of the closeness throughout history of the Normans and the Burgundians. After the evacuation at Dunkirk, Hitler stood on the French shore looking over the English Channel toward England. Observers rationalized Hitler was planning his invasion: or was he pondering why England had not made any of the moves that they had discussed earlier? Did Britain say something that would allow Hitler to think that they had joined forces somehow or that they (Britain) were interested in joining the new German Empire? As time went on Germany went about occupying its new possessions and seriously considering expanding the Empire. Prior to the war, Hitler had signed the pact of non-aggression with Stalin in order to prevent a repeat of the First World War, fighting on two major fronts.

Another unexplained event was why the Germans bombed London so heavily. Had Hitler finally realized that the British had deceived him and had changed their mind about joining forces, and did he concentrate his rage on London as a result? Why did Hitler's second-in-command, Hess, fly to Britain if not to re-establish the alliance or to find out why the British had not complied with previously held talks?

Interestingly, the Second World War was almost a repeat of the First. The fight started with the big three Germanics and mid-way through, the others (most importantly the U.S.) were drawn into it. While Hitler was expanding his new empire, thinking that Britain was going to join him, the British managed to get the U.S. and Russia involved. When Hitler realized that Stalin had back-stabbed him, Hitler vented his rage in that direction. He was now in the same position as the Kaiser several decades earlier. The U.S. had firmly declared that they did not want to get involved in this conflict; however, the Japanese had designs on the Pacific, most of which was controlled by the U.S.

Hitler saw his empire expanding around the world through the help of the Japanese, possibly even pressuring North America from both sides. All of this came together through what can only be described as the most aggressive act to date by the Moderns because of their inability to live peacefully. Britain had managed to pull off the same play as in the First World War with the help of the United States and Russia; as an added bonus their old enemy France got thumped in the process. A curious development of France's current dilemma was Britain and the U.S. taking over most French colonial holdings throughout the world. Coincidence? We will see.

One thing that was conspicuously absent this time was chemical-biological warfare. Europeans had developed "new rules" for warfare and could now consider it to be truly "civilized" engagement. However, that didn't stop the development of the atomic bomb, and the use of it.

One of the actions that helped destroy the Nazis and Fascists was their anti-intelligentsia policy. Only two of Hitler's senior staff had university educations, because generally this aspect of society was oppressed and persecuted. Hitler and his Nazis were by and large poorly educated extremists. Nazism, Fascism, and Communism were doomed to failure because of their narrow-minded ideals and view on life.

At the end of the Second World War the "big three" would be essentially bankrupt because of this long and bitter dispute. The United States would emerge as the most powerful society in the world, mainly because of the large influx of immigrants from around the world, who would provide a variety of ideas and input into the still-developing nation, and not because of any superior military brute force capabilities.

* * *

After the Second World War, the countries still under colonial control finally had their chance to break free because Europe was completely broken. In most of Africa, the Middle East, and India, right down through Southeast Asia, countries set about declaring independence. Some would not actually gain full independence until the 1970s and 1980s.

This huge independence movement was treated quite lightly in most history books. They explain how the colonial powers were committed to establishing or helping to establish self-government in the colonies. Scholars of the time insist that the Europeans really did not have a choice, and that their weakness, caused by the Second World War, was the opportunity the colonies needed to break free of oppressive European rule. They neglect to say that, given a choice the colonies, would boot the Europeans out in a heartbeat to finally be rid of them.

Europeans did their best to maintain some form of control over the newly independent countries; many of the brutal civil wars and conflicts that developed, particularly in Africa, were the result of continued European interference. That interference still exists.

* * *

Shortly after 1945, tension between the Western powers and Russia increased and the "Cold War" began. The primary reason for its growth and nurture was all the back-stabbing that had occurred in the years leading up to the Second World War and during the War itself. Stalin first sided with Hitler and signed a pact of non-aggression, and Germany and Russia began discussions on dividing up Poland and the Baltic states (again). After Hitler realized that Stalin had back-stabbed him, he launched a major offensive on Russia. Stalin then looked to the West for help, but it didn't come, because the West had not forgotten about his pact with Hitler, even though they said they were going to help Stalin.

When the Germans were defeated and the West and East met at Berlin, the Russians fully expected the Allies to keep going, and the Allies expected the same. Stalin had not forgotten about the broken promise of the Allies, who had never intended to help Russian, right from the beginning. A bitter stalemate ensued. The plan was to get Germany and Russia embroiled in conflict in which they would destroy each other. That did not happen. Instead it only strengthened the resolve of the Russian people and made Communist Russia much stronger. Once again, the Western countries blundered and created an even bigger problem.

(The following paragraph was added in 2006).

Some evidence that is just surfacing now is shedding new light on the relationship between Churchill, Roosevelt and Stalin. There is plenty of film footage showing them together strategizing to defeat the evil Nazis. However, it is now known that they each had their own agenda. Churchill and Roosevelt often kept each other in the dark because they both had plans to take over much of the occupied Nazi territories, after the Nazis had been defeated. Churchill was convinced that he could either befriend, or persuade, Stalin (a ruthless killer of millions of people) to divide these territories with

Britain, leaving the U.S. out in the cold. Churchill was obviously aware of the increasing power of the U.S.

In the years following the Second World War, Europe rebuilt itself, oddly enough led by Germany (again) and a new prosperity began to emerge based on capitalism and materialism. Cheap oil from the Middle East was the primary catalyst for the huge surge forward for the emerging Western democracies. Europe was finally getting along after 1500 years of continuous conflict and eventually established the European Economic Community (EEC) in 1957.

Why the Germanics (English, French, and Germans) fought and slaughtered one another constantly for 1500 years is a bit of a mystery. It's a given that they were pure barbarians who could not understand a structured society like those of the Greeks and Romans. Even the Greeks could not get along and fought continuously, even though they had a better grasp of the concept. The only logical explanation is that all Moderns lack the ability to be self-sufficient and are out of balance with their surrounding environment and evolved to be very efficient exploiters.

There's an interesting dynamic that seems to play a major role in the years leading up to the First World War, and, in fact, throughout the history of Europe. Europeans are very big on taking sides, and everybody has to be on a side, making it very difficult to stay neutral. The objective is to get others on your side because the more you have on your side, the better your chance of winning. This is largely because of the Europeans' inability to walk away independently. The English are the biggest abusers of this peculiarity...they always have to have somebody on their side.

It's very similar to what happens on a playground among children. Whether they're playing a game or simply arguing about one of life's small injustices, they have to choose sides. There are usually two sides, and everyone has to be on one or the other. Most of the conflicts that occurred throughout European history seem to manifest themselves in this manner. The only difference was that the leaders of the European countries were playing a bigger game. They were still just little boys choosing sides, but the stakes were higher.

The sad part about this behavior is that they insisted on including everyone else in their brutal squabbles.

* * *

Europeans now had to rebuild with less help from the colonies, upon which they had relied so heavily for centuries for support. The U.S. helped in this rebuilding through loans and the sale of American ingenuity, which gave them more control over European affairs, and access to their markets. The Japanese restructured their entire society and with even more Western-oriented philosophy they quickly became an economic powerhouse, but that was only temporary.

One black spot for the West was Korea. Japan had occupied Korea in one form or another for many years and full-time since 1910. After the Second World War and the defeat of the Japanese, the Russians took control of the north half and the U.S. control of the south. Under Soviet influence the North developed a communist regime and the South, not surprisingly, an anti-communist government under U.S. protection. Although the U.S. always tried to make it appear as though they were never *directly* involved in South Korean affairs, they were quick to step in when the conflict began. Each side had designs to reunite Korea under its respective political system. The North attacked in 1950 and the Korean Conflict began. The U.S. responded in aid for the South; a stalemate was the result in 1953. So, instead of Korea being able to move ahead on its own, now that the Japanese had been kicked out, the result was, once again, outside interference resulting in conflict.

Vietnam would suffer much the same fate.

Colonialism gave way to international trade as the former colonial countries sought to do economically what they had been doing physically. The new world order, led by the United States, allowed aggressive capitalism to expand and dominate the world markets. The Western countries could no longer rely on physically occupying their neighbors and so had to rely increasingly on economic supremacy. The former colonies around the world either had to play by Western rules or be shut out. Many faced *economic sanctions* if they did not follow the rules, and since the U.S. and Europeans invented the system in the first place, they held a definite advantage.

Most of the political grandstanding done by Western politicians about human rights and human rights abuses is a smoke screen for their real objective, which is to continue to dominate the world, one way or the other. Oddly, despite all their rhetoric about independent governments, the British were very reluctant to let go of India and Pakistan. Eventually they had to withdraw, and South Asia today remains a very tense trouble spot. In 1962 India and China were officially at war because of Tibet.

The Cold War was as much about breaking Russia's hold on countries that were potential markets as it was to crush "communist evil". The stalemate almost came to an end in 1962 during the Cuban missile crisis. Cuba had been under direct U.S. control for most of the twentieth century and was more or less a playground for wealthy Americans. In the 1950s Havana was one of the wildest places on the planet, and if you had the money to buy it, you could find it in Havana. The island people were badly treated and exploited. As a result, an anti-American force expelled the U.S. and their businesses. Cuba experienced much the same exploitation as China and needed an aggressive regime to keep the U.S. out. That hostility still exists, as the Americans haven't forgotten being beaten by a small guerrilla force and losing many years of exploitation and profit.

As more and more countries sought their independence and established their own governments, many sought out communism in preference to being taken over by aggressive capitalists. Since the Second World War the Western countries, led by the U.S. have portrayed communism as an evil, and by applying pressure and escalating the arms race they could get countries like Russia to use up most of their resources. They could then point fingers at the poor living conditions and apparent human rights abuses. The objective was to make sure that the communist system *failed*. When Vietnam started to adopt a system based on communism, the U.S. decided to intervene directly and physically to see if they (U.S.) had the resources and ingenuity to crush communism by force in a smaller country. We all know the outcome.

This seemingly useless war created a major social shift in the powerful Western democracies that has now largely been forgotten, but unknowingly put the Moderns on a new path.

For the first time in the history of the Moderns, huge segments of the population stood up and said, "War is wrong," and "Killing is wrong."

These long-haired peace-lovers, known as *hippies* changed the course of history. Many will argue that it was a phase that came and went, and that most hippies now are suburban taxpayers who are more concerned about garbage pickup than war. By and large, that may have been the case, but the seed was sown, and slowly continues to grow and influence younger generations.

Evolution is a painfully slow process.

* * *

Over the last 100 years or so, the Western powers would become, unknowingly, totally dependent on fossil fuels to sustain their economies. Westerners were finding a new freedom that they had not experienced before, as the automobile became more affordable. In the 1940s, 50s and 60s millions of miles of roads were built and everything and everyone relied on the gasoline- or diesel-powered, piston-driven forms of locomotion to transport goods and people to wherever they needed to go. The economy was booming because of cheap oil from the Middle East and the oil by-products refined afterward.

The piston-driven engine was essentially obsolete by the middle of the twentieth century. Other technologies and energy sources were being actively researched, such as electric, compressed carbon dioxide, and solar power. The point is that the piston-driven engine was kept in use when it should have been replaced, and the reason was cheap oil from the Middle East.

This dependence is now causing much of the world's conflicts and problems, not to mention monumental environmental destruction.

As the Middle East broke free of European control, it found itself struggling to maintain its freedom from the emerging superpowers, the United States and Russia. These two would require huge amounts of oil to maintain their economies, as almost every product bought or consumed by Westerners is processed from or has an oil base. Add to that the Cold War military buildup.

In the early 1970s the Middle Eastern countries managed to forge an alliance, which resulted in the Organization of Petroleum Exporting Countries [OPEC], but they made a crucial mistake. Shortly afterward the international price of oil began to rise and new controls were put in place; some Western countries found themselves a bit short on fossil fuel and paying a little more, and their new freedom was curtailed.

The western countries became "more involved" in Middle Eastern affairs and began to apply the old standard, divide-and-conquer technique, as one side was played off against another. The two primary targets were Iran and Iraq.

Some of the Middle Eastern countries were being indirectly controlled by the United States and Britain to ensure a constant supply of oil. Islamic fundamentalists overthrew the Shah of Iran and the Ayatollahs replaced the government. Shortly after that Iraq became increasingly hostile and the two (Iraq and Iran) went to war. It is widely accepted that the U.S. was the reason for this conflict because as the U.S. lost their control of Iran and the Shah, they gained control of Iraq and its government. It is also widely accepted that it was the U.S. who put Saddam Hussein in power as an ally who could now turn on Iran and, if they were successful in defeating Iran, the U.S. would control most of the oil reserves.

If the flow of oil stopped tomorrow or was even significantly reduced, the Western economies would collapse immediately. In 1973, when OPEC raised the price of oil more than 200 per cent, it immediately halted the forward momentum of the Western democracies.

That forward momentum was not just the economy; it also directly affected the social aspect of life as the continuous development of social programs also slowed. All socio-economic development of the Moderns relied on money and the continuous manufacturing and selling of consumer products, all of which are affected by oil and its use.

The Industrial Revolution greatly expanded the concept of materialism or commercialism, which has been around since Roman times and even before. I think we have managed to advance far enough so that personal or material possessions are not considered (at least by most people) to be more important than human life itself—or have we? We will talk more about this in the next chapter.

PRESENT DAY

So, here we are, still muddling along as the supreme intelligence. I hope readers have a clearer understanding of what happened to the human race. First, we adopted an aggressive behavior that was not *natural*. It would be misused, and not fully understood or controlled in many cases. Secondly, as humans evolved and went their separate ways, their development was influenced by many factors: when they splintered, from what group they splintered, their surrounding environment, and what groups they met and associated with along the way and either shared or stole ideas from. This is how the peoples of the world became so different from one another.

As the population expanded, groups came closer together and at some point they met. Generally speaking, the closer the proximity, the more aggressive the behavior. Many of them would meet during the Roman Empire. The most aggressive groups would dominate from that point onward.

Typically, as you move farther and farther out from the epicenter of "civilization", the Roman Empire, humans become less aggressive. The native people of the Americas, and of many other outlying regions of the world, developed in isolation from the more aggressive Moderns. This separation, combined with the surrounding environment, led to the development of a much different and more *self-reliant* culture. History has tried to portray these people as "savages", but it was not until the rest of the world forced themselves on these outlying cultures that they retaliated and rejected the aggressors' unknown, distasteful, dependent, and biased way of life.

The reverse is also true. The closer one gets to the epicenter of "civilization", the Roman Empire, the more aggressive the behavior. The individual groups were different from one another and this center was probably where the first splinter groups formed and dispersed. From the beginning, the various groups were in conflict with each other and splintered mainly because of internal squabbling.

When several individuals left they quickly found that none of them had the initiative to make their new group fully independent. These groups would remain in proximity to exploit each other, while other more independent and less hostile groups would continue to move to avoid the aggression.

Eventually and inevitably, they would run out of room. So, it would be the most aggressive, and least self-reliant groups, who formed "civilization" from that point onward, which is partly why every part of modern society today relies on every other part to function.

Right from its inception, civilization has been primarily based on one group of Moderns forcibly occupying another group. It is generally considered that Mesopotamia was, if not the first, one of the first settlements comprised entirely of Moderns, and it was there that this dynamic actually showed itself in the form of recorded "history".

Other Moderns descended on Mesopotamia which split into Assyria and Babylon. They in turn went on to be assimilated by other Moderns.

The first Greeks established themselves on the Mediterranean shortly thereafter, and eventually the Minoan society flourished. The Minoans were assimilated by a more aggressive Mycenaean society, which then split into several city-states. The most aggressive of these, Sparta, eventually disrupted most of the rest. The Macedonians then incorporated all of the states under their control and tried to conquer and assimilate the Persians. The Romans assimilated everybody, being undoubtedly the most aggressive of all groups to date. The Romans and the peoples they assimilated were then overrun by the Germanics.

The Romans would really paint a good picture of themselves and the idea of dominating other people and getting them to do all of the things that they, the Romans, could not or would not do just came naturally to them. *The Romans were the most dangerous people ever to walk on the face of the planet.*

From that time onward, the concept of using other people to get ahead and stay ahead of everyone else would become the standard. When Europeans came to the Americas and colonized other parts of the world with this in mind, they had no idea of the destruction they were about to unleash on the world.

Aggression begets aggression. When the Western Roman Empire crumbled, it was the most aggressive non-Romans who filled the void and continued in their footsteps.

It is quite likely that many Moderns right from the beginning, hundreds of thousands of years ago simply relied on taking out of the environment whatever they could, and did not develop the ability to utilize and adapt to their surrounding environment.

It is also quite possible that the people of the Americas and other outlying regions got there simply by trying to avoid these more aggressive groups. If you do not like your neighbor, you move. The irony in this is that the more aggressive people would eventually follow thousands of years later.

Moderns could also be referred to as *dependants* because they depend on everything being provided for them. Today they depend on water, electricity, building materials, food and public services to be provided for them to ensure their survival as they see the environment as being unimportant to them. Over time, the environment has taken quite a beating because the dependents continued to exploit and destroy it with little regard for anything except themselves. It seems as though the more "civilized" one is the more the environment suffers. This is quite a paradox because the environment is what has sustained the human race for millions of years, and continues to do so—for now.

Thousands of years of misguided aggression are directly responsible for many of today's problems. As we face the third millennium, we face many of the same problems as the Roman Empire. Citizens of modern democracies do not have to worry about a centurion coming along and lopping one's head off, although there are some Third World countries that still face similar problems because of the destructive setbacks caused by the colonial system.

Students of history and the human race quite often refer to the beginning of civilization as the beginnings of a complex society and as time went on society became more complex. This is an accurate description; however I hope it is clear by now that it was not because of any conscious effort on the part of Moderns. The reason we live in such a complex society is because we simply continue to add to a system that we never understood in the first place.

As people go about their everyday lives, they unknowingly live with many problems and fail to understand how and why these problems exist and keep recurring.

In Canada today, as well as many other developed countries, the legal and policing system are designed to protect society, our material possessions and our well-being. People who display aggressive behavior victimize many people. The aggression has nothing to do with being born "good" or "evil", but is the result of five million years of humans evolving through misguided aggression, oppression and losing the ability to be self-reliant, or never having it in the first place.

A major problem facing the human race is that it tends to live in the present and prefers to forget the past. In order to understand the present, you have to understand and face the past—not just the recent past but the whole past. And, along the way, many mistakes were made.

As humans evolved, they lost any natural instincts that they might have had while they were still primates. The result is that today, very few humans can exist being totally self-sufficient and probably 99.9 % of modern humans are dependent on society to provide for them in one form or another. Loss of our natural instincts has resulted in the need to rely more and more on learning capabilities. The human life cycle changed and the development period of infants extended so that they needed to rely on their parents longer than any other primates to increase the infant's learning time. Eventually human infants would be born with no normal instinctive abilities whatsoever and would be entirely helpless at birth. They required parental care for several years before being able to begin to look after themselves. The instinct to survive is perhaps the only natural ability left in humans.

Whatever knowledge and experiences infants gained along the way would determine their abilities and personality. Natural instinct was in part replaced by misguided aggression. Over thousands of years, aggression, in varying degrees depending on the individual, became part of human nature.

Over time, some humans have developed another ability called *human instinct*. I am not sure that I can fully define human instinct, except to say that it is an ability that makes some humans more perceptive to what is going on around them. Some people are just now becoming more aware of these instincts and are learning to follow their instincts. Women seem to have better human instinct than men do. Today some people can function using both learned intelligence and human instinct—unfortunately many seem to have poorly developed or non-existent human instincts. The Romans did not have human instinct and many people today lack good human instincts.

So, the modern human is a very complex creature because of our past history. Unlike most of the other highly evolved mammals, humans have developed a higher degree of intellectual variation. Some, according to human standards, are highly intelligent, but can lack human instincts. Others are the reverse and there is every combination in between. For example, if one was born with a genetic makeup that promotes the development of the right side of the brain, their instincts, the individual's parent care, education, and life experience until they are a young adult, would combine to essentially define that person.

An enormous number of combinations are possible. As a result, it appears as though whatever *stimulus* a human is exposed to from birth directly affects that individual's development because we no longer have any natural instincts to rely on and have become "conditioned" as we are generally force-fed information. It is quite likely that young humans need to be taught how to be non-violent to counter five million years of misguided aggression.

Things were further complicated 10,000 years ago when most humans went from hunter-gatherers to rural-urban dwellers. A combination of a poor diet, altered lifestyle and increased stress also has had an impact on development. From this point onward many factors come into play, such as one group intentionally destroying another group's food supply, as well as droughts and floods which naturally destroyed the only food humans had to rely on. Many died as a result and the rest would have to struggle on with just enough to keep them alive. Long-term effects caused our bodies, minds and general health continually to deteriorate.

As time went on, societies such as the ancient Greeks and Egyptians evolved with less outside interference and these Moderns were able to develop more progressive societies that were ahead of the other aggressive groups. Aggression was part of the ancient Greek and Egyptian societies, but as they developed more knowledge, awareness and understanding, aggression became less pronounced. This left them vulnerable to the less progressive but more aggressive groups.

At this point I would like to remind readers that when talking about human evolution you have to use generalities and focus on the big picture. Many readers are perhaps disagreeing with this perception of the human race because they do not have a spiteful or aggressive bone in their bodies and would never hurt anyone. Remember, there are varying degrees of aggression. Very few people consider all forms of life as important and would never consider harming anything. Others could never bring themselves to hurt another human being, at least physically, but would not hesitate to kill a wasp nest, a garter snake, shoot a deer or mentally torment another creature. These same people would support their government if they went to war and fully endorse their armed forces killing another country's armed forces. These are just varying degrees of aggression. In my opinion, our entire existence is based on exploiting the environment and everything in it and each other—and that constitutes aggression. Some people and some groups of people are clearly more aggressive than others.

The Romans were the first people in history to fully exploit others to their advantage. This would become the model because it showed that aggression and not necessarily intelligence could rule supreme. Evolution is a painfully slow process. Over time humans developed societies based on the ancient Greek accomplishments combined with Roman aggression. This is essentially how we got here.

* * *

Today we have to deal with many social and health problems, both physical and mental, and many people go about their lives thinking this is normal. More and more people are developing bone and joint problems, failing internal organs, bad backs and the list goes on. At the same time more and more people are being diagnosed with mental illness such as depression and schizophrenia, as well as other increasingly serious health problems such as allergies and diabetes. The list seems endless.

Add to these, five million years of misguided aggression and oppression and we are generally a pretty pathetic lot compared to when we were still hunter-gatherers.

If you added up all of the people suffering from one form of mental illness or another and compare it to the number of people who consider themselves normal, I think you might be shocked.

Mental illness is a fairly recent curiosity that has been getting more and more attention of late. Modern doctors are constantly identifying and classifying what they term to be new illnesses related to the mental well-being of humans. Many mental illnesses such as depression and schizophrenia have only been identified and studied quite recently.

Some doctors now think that as much as 30 per cent of modern societies, like Canada, either are depressed or are vulnerable to depression. Every year researchers isolate and categorize more and more mental illnesses. In a very short period of time I was able to find a list of about 70 illnesses relating to adults and their mental health. Many were individually estimated to affect approximately one per cent of the population with a likelihood of increasing that percentage in the future.

The insidious part about mental illness (and I think most doctors agree) is that most people are not aware that they are suffering from some affliction. They continue to go about their lives insisting that they are "normal". What is normal? Most people think they know, until they are diagnosed one day with an affliction and only then do they see mental illness in a new light.

While I was researching this area, an intelligent, perceptive young woman inquired why I was so interested in mental health. When I explained to her what I was doing, she replied, "There is no question that we all suffer from something."

The numbers have not really been added up yet, but I think if we try hard enough we could reach one hundred per cent.

Stress seems to be the latest obsession of the Moderns, who do not realize that stress has been part of civilization since its inception. People today who have more than one job or work more than 36 hours a week complain about stress. Stress has always been part of society; it just depends on what part of history you are talking about how much stress humans have or had. Moderns have to work in order to pay their bills. There is really no escape from it. If you have somewhere to live then you have to pay rent or a mortgage. You have to have food to survive because it is one of the basic elements of survival. The only way to get food generally speaking is to buy it, so you have to work to get food. Add to that, a list of secondary services that are required for your survival, like hydro bill, water bill, taxes, repairs, transportation, furnishings and the list is pretty lengthy. Most of these are necessary for Moderns to exist, and the only way that Moderns can live comfortably without any interruptions or hardships is to work. Every day you go to a job, where you perhaps have as many responsibilities as you do at home. All of these responsibilities are yours and yours alone and so the stress starts to mount or intensify. As the stress level intensifies you get physically and mentally rundown, and the more rundown you get the more the stress level intensifies. There is no break from your work, because you are only allowed a couple of weeks' paid vacation and so you have to work what seems to be all the time, without any break.

Personal problems worsen as perhaps a family member is sick or dies, but you cannot afford to take any time off work. You start to have trouble coping with either work or home life and it intensifies the stress and you have trouble concentrating. Before long you have too much stress and have trouble just coping with life in general, so your concentration at work starts to affect your work. Your home life becomes a disaster and your spouse dies or distances themselves and the burden seems overwhelming, and you don't remember to pay your bills and you are fired because you cannot do your job to your employer's satisfaction; except you are so rundown and exhausted that you can't find more employment; you can't pay your bills and the bank repossesses your house, you're evicted, and you become.... *homeless*.

Obviously we created most of the problems of present day in the first place.

Ironically people today are rediscovering some of the approximately 100 or more different plants that were used prior to farming in human diets as well as for medicinal purposes. I am not implying that modern medicine does not have a place in today's society, but because it now centers around the economy much of its benefits and potential are lost because of our need to make money.

Until recently, modern medicine focused primarily on the specific genetic makeup of humans as well as researching and producing vaccines that protect us from our little microscopic friends (which they may be if we understood them better). However, in the last decade, genetic research has (apparently) made leaps and bounds as scientists say, and the entire genetic makeup of a human is going to be mapped and understood. This has enormous implications for finding and possibly correcting previously incurable diseases. Scientists say that they will be able to isolate individual genes and that with their recent technology anything is possible.

As usual, there is a downside. As scientists race toward these revolutionary findings, private companies are racing to the patent office to patent as many individual genes as possible. Eventually private companies will probably own the entire genetic makeup not just of humans, but of every other creature. Any benefits that may occur in the future regarding human development probably will be controlled by private companies; nothing could be developed without their permission, thereby reaping enormous profits for them, probably at the expense of the human race as a whole.

The development of vaccines and their overuse, along with the complete sterilization of everything the health system uses, has had a reverse affect. Micro-organisms are becoming more and more tolerant and grow stronger because they can adapt. Our failure to understand them along with the unnecessary need to eradicate them has only made them stronger and they will come back with a vengeance. Currently hospitals are some of the unhealthiest places in society and the likeliest place to become sick. Fortunately many people are now much more aware of our poor state of health and are consciously trying to reverse this trend using more practical, natural methods. In the end, people will come to the conclusion that the only way to cope with our microscopic friends will be to be as healthy as possible because medicine and science may have failed us.

Stress, air and water pollution, and the accumulation of toxic chemicals in our environment aggravate the problem. For years, we watched these pollutants affect other highly evolved creatures yet set ourselves above them as though our supreme intelligence would somehow protect our biologically frail bodies.

* * *

Today, we have urban areas that rely on and are supported by farming communities much as they did 2,000 years ago. Currently there are very impressive modern machines to work farms, but despite our supreme intelligence many people, even in Canada, are not getting enough food to eat. Urbanites are in a quandary as children go to school hungry while there are hundreds of farms in provinces like Ontario that are going out of production. Many are being sold while people go hungry. What is happening? Where is our supreme intelligence? Why are farms going out of production less than two hours from Toronto, yet people do not have enough food to eat?

Modern farms in Canada are in great difficulty today, as the cost of farming has surpassed the income realized. Farming has become almost totally dependent on privately owned genetically modified crops and toxic chemicals. Most farmers are convinced that you would not be able to farm without chemical pesticides and herbicides.

Over several decades farming became a big business with millions of dollars involved in investment and operation, all in order to supply us with enough food to eat. Somewhere along the way the simple dynamic of rural areas growing food for the general population became somewhat skewed. As more and more processing companies became involved, the cost of food became more expensive. Eventually the government had to step in with subsidies to keep costs down, so that the cost of food (which is one of the basic requirements for survival) did not skyrocket beyond the reach of the average person. Today governments and banks, more or less, own and control most of the agricultural production (including farms) and at some point in the not-to-distant future, may have to assume full control to prevent the complete collapse of the industry.

Farming in Canada and elsewhere, has moved almost entirely toward science. Genetic manipulation [gm] allows the growing of "super crops" which are supposedly resistant to disease and insects as well as providing much increased yields or harvests. These genetically-altered species are sometimes referred to as "Frankenfood" because many people are now generally aware that there is something wholly unnatural about what is happening. These genetically modified foods were developed and introduced into our food stores without our knowledge, which opens the question, why? Were companies who stood to gain huge amounts of profit afraid we would reject them? Why are politicians so nave that scientists seem to be able to convince them that everything they (scientists) do is beneficial? Of course, a lot of it has to do with large private companies who constantly lobby governments and provide re-election dollars.

Most Canadians are totally unaware that the tomatoes they were buying had fish genes spliced into them and that is just one example. As this phenomenon becomes more public, the opposition to gm foods will grow. The gm supporters were hoping that they could convince the public that there was nothing to fear, *after* we ate these altered foods.

First I suppose we should define what is natural and what is potentially unnatural because there seems to be some confusion. Any plant species that reproduces in nature without human interference is natural. Even in nature, some species may occasionally produce a "hybrid", if they are similar enough to each other. If the hybrid is fertile and can then reproduce again then the hybrid makeup may continue naturally. If the hybrid is infertile then the reproduction process is halted naturally. Most hybrids have been found to be infertile and do not reproduce, and so nature controls this selective process. This dynamic happens in all aspects of nature such as fish and birds, not just plants.

So, perhaps we should be asking the question, if a tomato and a fish do not reproduce naturally should humans continue on this course? Just because they can do it, should it be done? Maybe nature knows more than we do. Historically, crossing the species boundary usually results in something negative or destructive. Currently, there are growing problems because of animal feeds which include by-products from several domestic animals, and diseases are now crossing species lines.

Most farms, at least in Canada, grow a very small variety of "cash crops", such as corn, soybeans, and canola. These are then sold to large processors who use them as a base to produce the variety of products that we see on our supermarket shelves. So, instead of these foods going directly from the field to our tables, they must first go through some process that is supposed to be beneficial when in reality it is merely a money-making process. These companies provide us with little more than processed "mush" and then have to *add* vitamins and minerals in order to meet nutritional requirements.

The narrow path that farming has taken has resulted in what is referred to as "mono-cropping". This simply means that there is a lack of diversity throughout the agricultural system. The Moderns are just now discovering that a lack of diversity produces some downfalls such as large losses due to disease. Nature and evolution provide diversity. Moderns know very little about nature, and the narrow genetic path they are on is getting narrower.

Out on the farm, chemicals are sterilizing the soil as farmers pour tons of pesticides and herbicides on the land. Soil is supposed to contain billions of microscopic bacteria and other forms of life to provide a continuous breakdown that decomposes organic material. That is what makes soil. Chemicals are killing much of this microscopic life and so soil is becoming simply a medium to grow "Frankenfood" which then requires tons of fertilizer or genetic manipulation to promote growth. Seems pretty self-destructive.

Some agricultural production turned into large businesses; the tobacco industry was the first giant to stagger. The governments of the Western world were willing to turn a blind eye to the increasingly detrimental effects of nicotine-manipulated cigarette products. This industry is a prime example of modern society. An increasing demand for profit resulted in the destruction of what was a viable industry, and governments let as many people die as they could to allow the industry to be viable. Eventually the health costs outpaced the viability of the industry and only then did government react.

What started out to be a harmless ceremonial practice by the Ancients… well, you know the rest.

The questions raised here will probably generate many different opinions. My theory is that our complex society is perhaps a little too complex for us.

* * *

About 500 years ago, wealthy European families began to establish trade and commerce. They dominated the economy for many years while governments tried to define exactly what their role was in all of this. Until the Industrial Revolution, the wealthy elite ran things and the common people served them. During the Industrial Revolution the lower classes had opportunities previously unavailable to them. A few became *entrepreneurs* and the concept grew. The main objective of this enterprising group was to do whatever it took to succeed. This was, and still is, the basic principle.

Let us briefly define what an entrepreneur is, because many people who are self-employed mistakenly put themselves into this group. As I see it, an entrepreneur has been, and continues to be, a person who basically personifies the concept of capitalism. An entrepreneur is totally devoted to starting, developing, running, and expanding a business or businesses. An entrepreneur does this with little regard for the human factors such as employees or competitors. An entrepreneur learns what is legal and what is not and pushes the envelope as far as possible to achieve success. Once an entrepreneur has attained a certain level of power and influence, then anything that may be illegal can easily be lobbied to become legal. A true entrepreneur has no morals. That is the difference between a person who is self-employed and an entrepreneur.

Over time the wealthy families and the entrepreneurs developed a closer relationship and many entrepreneurs strived to join the wealthy elite. This was their ultimate goal because it set them above many other humans. Oppression can also be a very strong motivator.

During this time governments seemed to have little input into social development and seemed to be preoccupied with waging war on other countries. Perhaps this was at the request or insistence of the wealthy elite for their best interests; they *were* the economy and the society and the poor were exploited to the extreme and the ones who actually got to be in the wars and conflicts.

My intention here is not to belittle the contributions of war veterans, both those who survived and those who did not. I am just trying to point out that in many instances throughout history the people who survived or died in these brutal conflicts between countries may have done so for reasons other than what they were told. Historically, many wars between Europeans started over little more than an insult uttered by a monarch or politician, but it would be rather naive, uneducated people who would ultimately pay the price. The common people were exploited for centuries and in many ways still are.

As the wealthy elite progressed, they developed into what is now known as "Big Business", which currently runs the global economy. This group is comprised of all of the largest companies and financial institutions. They invest money to make their businesses larger.

The governments' role in social affairs and improvement increased over time, largely due to increasing pressure by the working-class people. Today governments establish and control all social and public services using tax dollars collected primarily from the working people.

By the beginning of the twentieth century the concept of "small business" had been firmly established throughout the Western world, and today it is estimated that 90% of Canadians are employed by small businesses. Starting with the Industrial Revolution, the working class experienced periods of unemployment due to the introduction of machines. A solution to the problem was needed and self-employment flourished. Many people become entrepreneurs or self-employed during periods of high unemployment.

Many people will mistakenly try to argue that this is a good example of human intelligence, ingenuity, and progression when it is merely a quick solution to an unforeseen problem. This is how our modern Western societies have developed and still are.

Today society is essentially made up of three components, at least in Canada: Big Business, government, and small business/common people. Big Business essentially controls the global economy. Currently there are trillions of dollars in global assets controlled and manipulated by Big Business. Millions of dollars are exchanged around the world every day through the stock markets and other mediums. In any one country, this group is the minority.

Small business and working people make up the vast majority of the population. For centuries there were only two groups, the rich and the poor. The rich exploited the poor because, in their minds, they (the rich) were superior. The only regulating body in this period was a monarchy, which was generally a wealthy family with a King or Queen in charge. It is not difficult to see whose side they were on most of the time.

Over time governments would replace the monarchy in dealing with the day-to-day affairs of state. Eventually ordinary citizens would hold public office and the government, partly by pressure and partly because there were now people more sympathetic to the common people, would slowly begin to improve life for the average person. Today life is considerably better than two hundred years ago, but has the system changed any?

The majority of people who work for small businesses pay taxes and these tax dollars are collected by the government, which uses the money to improve social programs and establish new ones. The community is then, one hopes, improved, or at the very least, the system is maintained. We continue to provide tax dollars that come back to us as health care, education, roads to drive on, garbage collection and those sorts of things needed to create a happy community. The working people support themselves while Big Business continues to run the global economy and entrepreneurs and the very wealthy do what they always have, which is make more money.

The government's job is to keep both sides happy. This summary may seem very simplistic but when everything is stripped to the bare bone it is generally how society works. It is almost as though we, the people, are here only to provide the wealthy elite with manpower, for war and someone on whom to impose their will. Otherwise, we are pretty much on our own.

After the collapse of the Roman Empire, much of that system also collapsed and in fact did not resurface until recently. For several centuries life was based on poor and rich people. The rich people owned land and the poor people worked it and so land was the only thing of any value until the current economy began to emerge.

Whenever Big Business or anyone who collectively holds a certain economic interest wants to influence politicians and make their interests known, they do so by what is termed *lobbying*. A lobbyist representing a particular interest group approaches the government and attempts to influence politicians. In countries considered to be non-democratic, this is called corruption. All of this I call hypocrisy, which is something that Western countries are very good at. It goes hand in hand with covering up mistakes.

Maybe the "corrupt" Third World countries are only emulating what they see because many of these cultures were based primarily on observation.

The Canadian government currently has an official policy whereby any elected government that loses power and is replaced is not held accountable for *anything* that government did while in power. This hand-me-down from the British ensures that any mistakes or covert actions that the public is unaware of, is effectively buried by the former government as well as the current government. Much of it gets conveniently categorized as "National Security". One of the things that governments in many countries have become very good at and continue to be, is hiding the truth and covering up mistakes. This is, by the way, what has sparked the recent concept of *conspiracy theories* that is so prevalent today.

* * *

During the Roman Empire, the Greeks expanded the concept of *written law* and the legal system. This was added to over time, and this is generally the same system we use today. As civilization evolved, people would establish laws and rules that society should follow. This was the direct result of not having a well-established culture, because the cultures of the Ancients had natural codes built into their makeup. The Moderns, who developed "civilization", lacked this and so had to *consciously establish their morals and values*. As time went on civilization would find numerous ways to get around or exploit these rules; we continue to do so today.

Napoleon introduced the first police force in human history, the *gendarmerie*. Its primary function was to protect the wealthy and large landowners from poor people who were starving. Today, the police forces are still trained in a military style, which inevitably creates as many problems as it solves. Aggression begets aggression. The role of the police has evolved to also encompass the common people, because they now needed to have their material possessions guarded and when their services are required, the police in most instances assume a confrontational posture. Most ancient cultures did not need a police force or a paid army.

The system has changed very little in the last 500 years and requires that the people who display aggressive behavior be locked up in cages (jails), much like animals in a zoo. The sad part is that perhaps some of these people *need* to be locked up in cages because of thousands of years of aggressive behavior, and I am not suggesting that we let them out tomorrow.

Unfortunately there is another sector of society that is treated similarly but the causes are from a different source. Many people who "act out" in an aggressive manner do so because they have difficulty dealing with, and understanding, modern society and its oppressive and rigid form. Combined with a natural tendency to want to be more independent and follow their own instincts, they are looked down on and often even feared. Many end up outside of society, partly because they choose to be, and partly because society pushes them out. Many of today's youths fall into this category. Over the last 2,000 years society has been based on exploiting other people and breaking their wills rendering them submissive to the aggressors. As young people mature through puberty and develop individual identities and grow in self-reliance and begin to follow their instincts, people and society feel the need to break their wills in order for them to become "useful and obedient" members of society. Children as young as two years of age begin to develop their own identities; in some cases, young people's instincts tell them that there is something fundamentally wrong with what they are taught, as quite often what they are told does not mesh with what is actually happening. Many simply refuse to be "conditioned". Over the last 2,000 years many people who displayed good human instinct were branded as "witches" and "heretics" and burned at the stake or killed some other way. This has only slowed the evolution of the Moderns.

The idea of universal education is fairly recent for the emerging Western democracies. Previously only the wealthy received any official tutoring and the majority of people knew only the very basics, and most could not even read or write. As more and more common people entered into public service, they realized how much was lacking in this area and the current education system began to develop. In the new country of Canada, there was considerable conflict between Protestants and Catholics and each developed their own school system. Catholics insisted on maintaining control over those who were devoted to their faith and Protestants pushed for a public school system. Until very recently each system fully imposed their religious ideals on young people who attended their schools, and many are still trying to maintain religious aspects of life in the school system.

As I was growing up in a predominantly white, Protestant background, in the 1960s and 70s, we were taught not only readin', writin' and rithmetic, but also that we were Christian, Protestant, and that we were still the Queen's subjects. Pictures of Her Majesty adorned every classroom and young people said "The Lord's Prayer" and sang "God Save the Queen". Half of our education was based on living in Canada and learning about Canadian history and society, while the other half was devoted to ensuring my loyalty to a Protestant Queen and Great Britain. This was incredibly contradictory and confusing, as I was always under the impression that Canada was an independent country that had been a colony of Great Britain many years ago. So the public school system taught Protestant values and the Catholic separate schools, Catholic values.

Along with Canadian, British, and United States history, we were also taught that Canada, the U.S. and the British Empire were the "most civilized" countries and that we lived in "civilization". The words *civilization* and *democracy* kept recurring at regular intervals and over time many fellow classmates and I believed that we were somehow superior to many other people. Many other cultures were excluded from my education, and so I was ignorant of these other cultures and societies until I took it upon myself to correct the problem.

As time went on and I began to pay more attention to world affairs, I realized something was wrong. Every time I turned on the television there were people being killed: in Northern Ireland, Vietnam, the Middle East, Africa, or somewhere else. Something did not seem right and I began to question things. For reasons that often did not seem to be very civilized or intelligent, we (the civilized ones) seemed to be doing much of the killing. Over time I realized that in effect our upbringing was really just a form of 'conditioning' because humans rely almost entirely on learning as they grow to adulthood (I hesitate to use the term brainwashing because it implies that it was done maliciously). We were taught that we were civilized, superior and to stay loyal British subjects. Why? Are they afraid that, given a choice, I would not want to be Christian, Protestant, and loyal British subject? I only wanted to be a good human.

There comes a point where it becomes very difficult to reverse the conditioning of a human. Because of our reliance on learning, deprogramming involves the whole educational process.

As young humans grow they are taught whatever the adults think is necessary to be "productive", but is it a complete picture? As soon as infants are aware of their surroundings, most begin to show a fascination with nature and all of the other strange and wonderful creatures that surround them. Most children show some interest in nature and many seem drawn to it almost instinctively. They show incredible delight and curiosity about frogs, insects, birds, and anything else that moves—and also much that doesn't move such as trees, and plants. When children start school, their curiosity about nature is taken away because the Moderns do not see that as being important or having any bearing on what profession or trade children might take. So they are conditioned to shun nature and the other creatures that inhabit the planet.

Then something else happens that has a major impact on young humans. Puberty. Humans can reproduce at around 13 years of age, yet aren't considered fully grown (physically) until 21 to 23 years of age. That is about ten years of reproductive capability with very little guidance, as many parents still refuse to discuss these topics with their children. This becomes quite a dilemma as young humans move through and past puberty and their main focus becomes socializing and the opposite sex. Most spend their entire waking day obsessed with this new and unknown phenomenon, and so learning becomes less important.

It is not entirely clear why humans evolved in this way, but the Ancients' cultures seem to have solved the problem, while the Moderns still struggle with this even today. Many ancient cultures considered this period a sign of young adulthood and began the process which would lead to (hopefully) a mature adult. They then spent a considerable amount of time and energy guiding these youths through the next ten years. Moderns, however, still don't know how to deal with this problem. Moderns set an arbitrary age (which can change at will) of anywhere between 18 and 21 when young people are supposed to start being an adult (albeit a maladjusted one). On that birthday, you're an adult.

Add to all of this, a constant stream of biased information from the education system which young people do not understand, but memorize and regurgitate just to please adults.

As young people grow and are conditioned they are under the impression that there is a wonderful future ahead of them in civilization. As they go through secondary school they realize that this, in fact, may not be the case. Many of the adults they know, including their own parents, are under tremendous stress, because of the global recession, downsizing, closures, layoffs; many students themselves cannot even find low paying jobs. So we are still providing a basic education that many are finding totally useless to them. Some will strive to attend college or university but even this is becoming out of reach for many. When they watch the news they constantly see university graduates who are unemployed with no prospects of a job. Society is going through change.

* * *

All of this force-fed information is designed to condition young people and then to slot them into society and the work force, the basic concept being that one must work in order to provide for oneself and to acquire material possessions. Many people aggressively strive to acquire possessions, as well as necessities to ensure basic survival. Those who quest for material possessions to enrich their lives continue to work very hard. So, we have managed to evolve far enough to at least ensure that a citizen receives the basic requirements, and society, at least in Canada, does its best to prevent a person from perishing. Pretty civilized.

You go off to work and perform your specified duties so that you can make a living and buy all of this amazing technology that is around you and that we are told will improve our lives. You also have to raise your offspring and provide everything necessary to ensure basic survival. While at work, you have to deal with many people, some of whom appear to be more aggressive than others are, and so you struggle to do your best. Some people who are not in positions of authority sometimes act like they are, or want to be, and many people strive for this more aggressive position. The problem is that most people in positions of authority have more aggression than compassion, skills and character. Work becomes the main priority and people are less important. The company is downsizing and you get laid off because the owner needs to make more money. You then realize that the company's need for more money is partly due to the need to stay competitive, because it is "pretty aggressive" out there, and partly because the owner and shareholders would simply like to make more profit and so this need apparently exceeds the importance of human life. But wait, that cannot be because…that is the way it was in Roman times.

Just forget I mentioned it. Just when you are getting ahead, all of the bills come in and suddenly you are not. Perhaps this is the meaning of life that so many search for.

As time went on, labor unions developed because ordinary people were being exploited by the rich and powerful. They aggressively fought for more and more rights for the worker. Eventually many would achieve these goals. Unionized workers today are making a very good wage for their labors, but over the past 20 years or so, unions have misused and exploited their new powers. Many unions are now under close scrutiny, have lost considerable strength, and have far more people in their ranks than they can effectively justify. So much of what was gained is now being transferred back to the government and the rich and powerful.

The common people who were exploited for decades finally had their chance, their moment to cast off the chains, but they blew it. It turns out that they are not so different from the people who were oppressing them. Human behavior is fascinating.

I would also like to point out here that no one is to blame because human behavior is universal.

Unfortunately many of the people in society, regardless of what they do for a living, will, at some point, try to take advantage of others or a situation. This is, in large part, due to the many years of Roman and colonial influence, and the system that developed from it. People go about their everyday lives, politicians as well as citizens, with ulterior motives while coming across as being sincere. Add to that the fact that we hate it when others get ahead of us and it makes for a pretty interesting life.

* * *

Another peculiar aspect of modern humans is that they all take credit for everything that happens or every time someone else accomplishes something significant. When a small group of humans put a man on the moon, or when someone invents a vaccine or cure for a disease, most people want to be there when the credit is handed out. If someone invents a device that makes life easier for the handicapped or for humans in general, we collectively want to take credit for it. When doctors perform heart transplants, we all want to take credit for it. I don't know about you, but I personally had nothing to do with putting a man on the moon and I did not transplant any hearts. We have a tendency to lump ourselves together whenever the term "intelligence" is used. That is not to say that people who do not work for NASA lack intelligence, but many people who are just plain ordinary folk seem to crave that type of accomplishment, although most will not achieve it.

It takes years of accumulated knowledge and study in a very narrowly-focused area to achieve great accomplishments. Someone who can transplant a heart may be totally inept at doing anything else. It takes many people, unlimited resources, and decades of intense study to achieve results. It seems we all want to be intelligent and so if the human race makes any type of advancement or if something new comes along, "we" did it. I suppose that the argument could be made that if we paid taxes, then we should share in the glory when it comes; but is that intelligence? Take away the financial resources that are required for these accomplishments and see what happens.

* * *

Our structured society is still based around a hierarchy and everyone fits into the hierarchy somewhere. It starts right from the moment you are born. You are in a hierarchy if you have siblings. Hundreds of years of conditioning have resulted in the older child dominating the younger ones who are expected to be submissive to everyone. All children are submissive to their parents and other adults. Each family has its pecking order, the direct result of a society that based itself on which class you were born into, birth order and family name.

Adults have their own hierarchy. Historically, poor people are expected to be submissive to wealthier people. Our entire society is based on many little hierarchies. When you start into the work force, you are at the bottom of the hierarchy, and so begin the slow climb to achieve the best position you can. Some people are able to get higher than others. Going from the lower levels into a higher level automatically entitles you to more prestige and respect; in effect, you see yourself as a better human being than those below you because of this accomplishment. The ultimate goal for many is to be at the very top.

The entire system is subject to many flaws of human nature. Some deliberately try to keep others from rising while others use aggression rather than skills and character to go higher. There are those who have no desire to climb the ladder and often resent those who do. I wonder what society would be like if each individual were judged on character, as opposed to a person's ability to make money and how much money they had. Again, this is the direct result of a people who historically lacked a well-established culture, and had to consciously establish their morals, values and social structure.

People in the work force are now realizing that they do not want to be submissive to someone else just because of their position in the hierarchy. In fact, many people are now questioning the whole concept of going to a place of employment to perform a specific duty, just to ensure one's survival.

Just recently many working-class people have been able to acquire luxuries that were not available to their ancestors. Many are now seeking more leisure time and resenting work more. They now realize that there is more to life than working and acquiring material possessions, which provide only short-term gratification.

Over the last 30 years or so many people have taken more control over their lives and workplaces, and are striving to reduce the workload expected of them while increasing their wages. Many people are just now realizing that working, even if it is something they are good at, does not always create fulfillment. So, it is becoming somewhat of a dilemma because one must work to achieve and maintain the lifestyle that we want.

It was during the Roman Empire that modern society began to take shape. The Moderns did not have the same broad-based knowledge that the Ancients had incorporated into their evolution. As a result many Moderns developed a specific trade or craft that they were good at, or at least performed well enough to make a living. Each person developed a specific talent and society developed a complicated system for utilizing each individual trade or craft. The objective was to do something that was in demand.

Eventually this complicated system would be entirely reliant on each segment of society functioning efficiently so that the entire system also functioned efficiently. If one of the dominoes fell, it could affect many of the other dominoes. It is a very precarious system that the Moderns have devised, a system that could have been the direct result of Plato's concept of a perfect society.

Over time Europeans would eventually reconstruct a similar system and the common people became the "working class". This working-class system was the direct result of the oppression of the poor people who were literally forced to work for the rich. The only option in life is to work hard to get out from under the oppression, but once we get out from under the oppression, the natural thing to do is to want to work less often and less hard (much like richer people). Unfortunately, the system is designed so that people have to work hard, and there has to be a hard working class for the system to function. *In this system even people have to be exploited for the system to function.*

People slowly realized that they no longer had to work hard to maintain a good lifestyle. As they slowed their personal production, thinking, "I don't have to work any more thanks to my union," the production of their company also slowed, and it became less competitive. People no longer equated working with income, and so their sole objective was just to retain their job because it still meant their survival and wanted to maintain their "standard of living". The concepts of "a job", "having a job", or "keeping one's job" became the primary concern to ensure survival. The result is a decrease in productivity, which eventually results in a loss of their job, when low productivity brings about the failure of the business.

In about the last 30 years working people in both the public and private sectors achieved a very high standard of living in Canada. Unions in both sectors were swelling their ranks and horror stories began to surface. Some of the larger unions were allowing memberships to increase to the point where each person was doing an absolute minimum of work on a daily level. Their members were also self-employed and sometimes were doing work for themselves on company time.

Unions and bureaucracies became so large that one person did not know what the next person was doing, or was supposed to do. In fact the objective that people seemed to be striving for was to receive a better than average wage without actually doing anything. Can this be viewed as moving toward a more self-reliant or self-sufficient society? Perhaps this is the Utopia that everyone looks for. How then can a system that requires people to work in order for it to function be maintained if this is the direction in which we wish we could go? Unions are quickly losing ground as the working people continue to demand an increase in wages, benefits and insist on a share of any profits the company may make. I'm afraid, as the global economy shrinks so does your standard of living.

During the same period special-interest groups, as well as many individuals concerned about social programs, put pressure on the government to provide more funding. Currently the education and health care systems are at the top of the list.

Over the past 40 years the Canadian economy has been very strong. We became accustomed to expanding and improving our lives by way of social programs. Many people were beginning to see a much more humane society that provided for all. Recently, Canada has experienced several recessions, and these programs have been cut back. Many people are outraged. In our dependent society, there are only X tax dollars that can be generated. When this money is gone many people still have concerns or expectations that just cannot be fulfilled and so we regress because of this. This Utopia that so many people are seeking and came very close to achieving is not about to appear in a system that relies *entirely on money.*

Immigrants coming to Canada also think it is a Utopia because that is the way Canadians portray themselves. Immigrants find a better standard of living, but many eventually realize that Canada, like other countries, is far from being Utopia. The government slots them into mainstream society as common working-class people, and they must also pay increasingly oppressive taxes in order to maintain one of the highest standards of living in the world.

Every social program relies on money to function. In fact, social progression and existence in Canada and every other Western democracy entirely relies on money and the continuous forward progression of the economy. All social programs dealing with crime and rehabilitation, helping the physically and mentally handicapped, education, health and, in effect, everything that defines modern society and how it develops is reliant on money. *Even our compassion relies on money.*

Every major study initiated, whether it is about Crown Land use or even the Constitution, is limited in length and scope and therefore progression because of money. When the economy is healthy, governments fulfill many of our expectations. When it is not, they do not.

* * *

Today, most of the world is experiencing a recession, much like several in the past, but this one is different. The system that has been running the global economy for the last 200 or more years is now obsolete. It was based around the Industrial Revolution and primarily manufacturing, exploiting the environment and people, and the use of fossil fuels. Everyone was very busy building the country over the last 150 years. Currently Europe is relatively stagnant and the economies of Canada and the U.S. are questionable and unstable, and, in fact, will remain so. None of them will rebound to levels previously seen.

Some industries will always be required because they produce goods and services that will always be needed. The high-tech industry is very specialized and does not provide anywhere near the employment opportunities that manufacturing did. There may be a slight resurgence produced by all of the now elderly baby boomers spending their money.

Many Western countries will now look toward the Third World countries as they finally emerge from being raped by the colonial system. Third World countries are just now starting to develop economies much like the Western Hemisphere has had for some time. These new markets will help to keep the economy going for a while. What happens when they come up to our level? Where then will we look to keep the Industrial Revolution rolling along in its wheelchair?

In the early 1990s, analysts following global economic trends were predicting that Asia (the Pacific Rim countries) would rule the global economy in the next millennium. In 1998 their economies had all but collapsed. That is because the global financial movers and shakers commonly manipulate imaginative pieces of paper, (which are supposed to be worth something) for so long then the house of cards collapses. Historically, trade and commerce was based on tangible things. Today most of the global transactions do not exist except on paper.

Stocks, bonds, mutual funds, and other paper is bought and sold every day without any tangible item ever changing hands. People invest, and are persuaded to invest, in companies that either do not yet exist, or have just been established and are expected to become large money-makers. In the 1800s, people who wanted to cash in on railway expansion created *speculation.* An economy cannot run on speculation.

Add to that the single-mindedness of developing high-tech and electronics and reshaping the entire economy based primarily on making TVs and VCRs. Japan's economy boomed in the 1970s and the 1980s because they made better TVs and stereos than anyone else. Inevitably everyone else would duplicate what Japan was doing and now everyone can make good TVs and stereos. Most of Japan's economy was based on producing electronics and they have since essentially lost their primary base, with nothing to replace it. Japan's economy went flat and will probably remain so, as the world market has become flooded with electronics. This process is still in motion in the high-tech arena. Manufacturing is receding and high-tech has reached its peak. Humans are only finding new ways to repackage the same technology, and eventually it will no longer be able to support the economy. Some people are confident that "something else" will come along; after all we are a supreme intelligence. It hasn't come yet.

The situation of modern Western democracies can be compared directly to the decline of the Roman Empire, just on a larger scale. As was mentioned previously, the Roman Empire became stagnant when everything happened within the empire's boundaries and it was no longer moving forward or expanding.

The same could be said about the current situation. The Western economies are faltering and so in order to keep them moving, they must continue to pressure everyone else to be like them. They have run into some problems. Many Third World countries are locked in chaos and confusion as they struggle between retaining their Ancient cultures and accepting a free-enterprise system that suppresses many of the old ways.

Russia proved to be a huge disappointment to Western states as the Russians seem to lack the ability to become "Western". After decades of Cold War neutrality and billions of dollars spent on breaking the communist system, the payback for Western countries has been dismal.

If Russia and the Russians had wanted to, or could, become Western, they probably would have by now.

The Eastern Bloc countries are so far behind that they may never catch up; North Korea is an economic disaster; that leaves China.

It's interesting that countries like the United States which so strongly opposed the communist system and Chinese human rights violations, are now putting on blinders just to get access to China as a potential market. If China opens its doors to the Western countries that may spur the global economy for quite some time.

Many people outside of the Western realm continue to resist Western ways; this inevitably causes the empire to stall and when it stops moving forward, the only option is to maintain, which eventually leads to decline.

* * *

In our reliant society we have a great deal of difficulty understanding the natural environment, partly because we evolved away from it. The environment was not incorporated into our very structured lives. This has caused much concern during the last 30 or 40 years. Many Moderns are now more aware of the environment and the destruction that humans are causing; however, evolution is a painfully slow process, and it is only when pollution is actually visible these humans react. In the 1950s and 1960s pollution started to show itself—it was only then that people raised concerns. The Great Lakes, bordering Canada and the United States, were frothing with phosphates and other human-made chemicals and smelled and looked awful and so people got upset. Garbage filled roadside ditches and when it looked untidy, we cleaned it up. All of this pollution was created by Moderns and much of it we cannot see.

This is what is referred to as *cause* and *effect*. We cause the problem and then we see our mistakes (effect) for which or are forced to find a solution. Most environmental problems are caused by industries that provide gainful employment. Since everyone needs to make money I think the dilemma is quite clear. If these pollutants and toxic chemicals get into our water supply and our bodies what is the point of having an industry or a job? So, we wait, until they appear, somewhere. If these chemicals affect our judgment, how will we know?

Our evolution away from the environment shows up in the simplest places. Many countries, such as Canada, are located in extreme latitudes and so the temperature often dips to -30C in the winter and rises to +40C in the summer. We tend to go about our everyday lives as though each day is a balmy spring day regardless of the outside temperature. The objective for many is to drive from one's heated or cooled garage to a heated or cooled parking area at work, thereby eliminating the environment. Many dependent people strive for this goal. Sadly this is partly due to the fact that people have to get to work even in temperatures which can be life-threatening and partly because many people do not even think twice about it. So controlling our environment has now become an important preoccupation with scientists, engineers and many others. They arrogantly think that now that they have created artificial environments inside, which still do not work, they can control all of nature and everything outside. How can they control something that they do not understand? Currently scientists are considering altering weather patterns in efforts to prevent natural events such as hailstorms at the insistence of large insurance companies. What they fail to understand is how fragile the environment is because it has been slowly evolving for billions of years. The environment relies on itself to keep this fragile balance; it can only take so much abuse and some mistakes are not easily correctable.

This has already happened over the past 2,000 years, as most of Europe and then North America, as well as other parts of the world, were largely stripped of their forest vegetation. Combined with all of the pollutants that go up from urban areas, this has altered the makeup of the atmosphere. In my opinion we have less oxygen to breathe than we did 100 years ago, and certainly much less than 500 years ago.

So, as we continue on our dependent way, we continue to be totally ignorant of how incredibly important the environment is to our existence. Instead of learning to live with it, we continue to fight against it because the majority of people do not know any other way. *Moderns have always tried to shape the environment around their society instead of shaping society around the environment.*

Of course the problem now is that most societies are still based on exploiting the environment and producing pollution. We stumble along dredging, backfilling, channeling and altering all of the natural waterways, arrogantly assuming that this is somehow better than what nature has done. Recently we have discovered that perhaps this is not the case, as many regions in the world are experiencing flooding and soil erosion. Most of the natural floodways and marshes are now backfilled and paved over and many rivers and streams have been straightened, or channeled, which only increases the water flow.

All of these things are not unique to Canada. All of the modern industrialized countries do much the same, and in the next ten to twenty years many humans will come to realize that they, in fact, cannot do it better than nature and do not fully understand its complexities and therefore should not assume that Moderns can duplicate or engineer nature.

Most of these problems are directly associated with urbanization and industrialization. Many of the developing countries are now poised to go through their own little industrial revolutions and so will only add to or extend these problems. Because of the destructive setback of the colonial system, developing countries are now forced to follow the developed world and go through the same destructive process.

The people of the Americas, prior to European arrival, never had to worry about these things as everyone's life was integrated with the environment around them. The Mayans were perhaps the only advanced human civilization to be fully integrated with the environment. So, as we start the next millennium, the human race faces many old and many new problems making people apprehensive as to what the future holds.

* * *

One of the really interesting, and most often overlooked, aspects of life and the history of civilization is that all of the chaos, war, brutality, killing and social problems can be directly blamed on *men*. Throughout the history of "civilization" it has been primarily men who have dominated the societies of the moderns, and so it is they who should also accept responsibility for most of the failings of society.

This domination started many thousands of years ago and came about simply because the male of our species is, generally speaking, physically stronger than are females. This is quite common for many species that inhabit the planet.

Unlike some creatures that nature has provided with natural instincts and helped to define the roles between male and female, human females were left entirely to the whims, desires, and neediness of human males. For reasons not yet entirely clear, men seem to think that they are superior to females.

Somewhere along the evolutionary path humans lost their instincts and, while they lacked instinct, they also lacked intelligence. Perhaps it was here that brute strength was the primary, or sole, asset of the human race.

Women were relegated to a cheerleader role and were ignored for the most part. But, as the females socialized back at camp, they had thousands of years to observe the men and watch all of their mistakes. I personally think that this is how they developed their "female intuition". Essentially they could be classed as outsiders, which is the best position from which to observe any situation. As time went on, women had to be very careful about making suggestions or suggesting change, as men's egos are easily bruised.

A prime example of male domination has already been mentioned, as women are quite often the initiators of change and probably discovered farming. By this time the gender roles were too deeply entrenched for women to be able to carry on with any type of change or idea and so society evolved through men's brains with some unrecognized input from women. The reason we live in a society of concrete, steel, and machines is because of this male domination. If there had been more female input into the development of civilization, society would be profoundly different and probably better. If you keep this in mind and reread history I think you will find that it was primarily men who started wars, caused hardship and famine, developed weapons to kill, and caused the death of millions of innocent people. There have been, and are some women who are willing to play by "men's rules" but they are few in number.

Recently researchers have been studying the concept of learning and have discovered that, generally speaking women are more intelligent than men, which comes as no surprise to most women. They are also studying why boys do better at subjects like math and science than do girls and why the two genders learn at different rates. In modern Western societies most men are left-brain thinkers, which apparently is primarily focused on logic, precision and mathematical equations. Einstein is probably the best example of a Modern male who mistakenly thought that life could somehow be explained through mathematical equations. Women tend to be more philosophically and socially oriented. They had also become very dependent on men, through no fault of their own, and are still struggling with a lack of self-confidence and still have a tendency to need security, but this is quickly changing. As we start the next millennium, women are playing more and larger roles in society but are still finding it difficult to break through male-imposed barriers. As women gain more self-confidence, they are finding that they do not need men or need to rely on men as they have always done. This is going to play a major role in the future. Many of the ancient cultures were much more tolerant of women and some were matriarchal (women were dominant) as opposed to patriarchal (male dominated). Perhaps we could learn something from the cultures that the Moderns are intent on destroying. Having said that, I personally have met a lot of women whom I would consider fairly aggressive and so just changing from a male dominated society to a matriarchy is probably not the answer. Will society be better with more women in positions of influence? Only time will tell. Perhaps somewhere in between would be more appropriate.

* * *

Currently there are still conflicts going on around the globe among various races of people, religions, and even economies. More and more people seem to be gravitating toward the concept of evolution, despite its having been around for a couple of centuries or more, perhaps because of the conflict (past and present) between various religions and even within the same religion. As we enter the new millennium, scientists and the religious communities are going head to head. The scientists insist they are firm believers in the theory of evolution and hope that their intense study of space will yield the results that they seek. The religious leaders still hold to the fact that scientists have yet to unlock the mystery of the universe and evolution and so one waits while the other looks.

All of the various Moderns of the world are still very much at odds with one another and each is perhaps wondering whose way is better or who will find the solution to questions such as the meaning of life or understanding life. Will it be the scientists? The wealthy elite? The common people? Democracy? Asians? Muslims? Biologists? Caucasians? Buddhists? Archeologists? Communists? Or Christians?

DENIABLE REALITY

Who do you suppose might hold the key for the Moderns in order for them to understand?

Well, the answer is *none of the above* because quite frankly if we could give every creature on the planet a type of universal intelligence test, my guess is that humans may not make it into the top three.

Something has been missing from this whole equation until now—the other forms of life that also live on this planet. It has been only in the last 30 years that the environment and all of its inhabitants have been noticed by modern societies. Prior to this only a few Moderns showed any concern for all forms of life. As the Moderns went about exploiting both the flora and fauna, they found that many of the original plants and other creatures that we evolved with are now either gone or near extinction. This is not to say that some of them were not destined for extinction, in fact many were, but the Moderns have unfairly sped up this process.

Over the course of millions of years many of the other mammals have also been evolving and because they are so different from us we have a tendency to ignore that fact, because of our physical abilities and different appearance. Moderns can build some very impressive things, and they mistakenly associate this with intelligence. We are just now beginning to realize that many of the other mammals show a remarkable degree of intelligence. Creatures such as whales and dolphins have been communicating with each other for thousands, and perhaps millions of years, in or under the water, and it is quite likely that creatures like dolphins not only communicate but are also *telepathic*, something that we humans only dream about. The fact that they do this in a different medium (water, not air) should not take anything away from this remarkable ability. It is quite likely that when dolphins make their cute little squeaky noises that we humans love, they are either trying to communicate with us or they are laughing at us, and we are not intelligent enough to realize it, or understand it.

When whales and dolphins are beached it is not just because of the tide, they are having their underwater lines of communications disrupted, as well as their sonar-location abilities. Many of the abilities that these creatures possess are only now being duplicated by Moderns *with machines* while the animals have been doing it for perhaps millions of years. Most of our ideas came from them. Many species, from whales (the sperm whale has one of, if not the largest brain of any mammal) to ants, and even some plants, show a remarkable degree of intelligence, but we just miss it. Many creatures have been persecuted throughout history because they have shown human-like qualities or intelligence. Wolves, ravens, coyotes, and the sperm whale (Moby Dick) are but a few and I am sure each reader can think of others.

Researchers have observed ravens doing remarkable things humans just cannot explain (or accept). Recently they have discovered that a raven's brain has an exceptionally well-developed front cranial area, and yet very few people seem to know or care that the raven is one of the most intelligent, hardy, and resourceful creatures on the planet. For years humans pondered the prospect as to whether or not other mammals think and reason. Well, they can, and it has been proven beyond a doubt, yet no one seems to care. We have known since the 1950s that ravens can identify numbers and can count. In many parts of the world the raven has been associated with the occult and evil for centuries. This was primarily due to its intelligence, and it may have shown even more intelligence than the people who condemned it. For decades researchers have been writing reports that circulate only within scientific circles, and never seem to generate broad interest. It has taken more than 100 years for the concept of evolution to gain acceptance, and it may take another 100 years for the Moderns to accept the fact that we may not be the most intelligent creatures on the planet. The fact that very few humans seem to care supports this idea, in an odd sort of way.

An article by Charles Wilkins in *Canadian Geographic* magazine reports that recently in Northern Canada, ravens were observed to intentionally loosen snow on metal roofs as humans walked underneath, and in fact, tried to hit them. One observer made note that ravens seem to have a sense of humor. I am not sure that was their primary intention; perhaps they were just disgruntled with the human race in general. In another reported incident, two ravens were seen easily outwitting a seemingly intelligent family dog. As one raven lured the dog to the backyard, the other flew in to help itself to the dog's food. They then reversed the roles and within a few minutes had an easy meal. The dog did not stand a chance. Ravens seem to be able to exploit any opportunity and have been seen intentionally soaking dry bread in water to soften it up before eating it. In fact, ravens seemingly have evolved along with us. In the wild they are very opportunistic and will feed literally on anything. They have an unusually close relationship with wolves and in the wild they seem to help each other. During the winter months they converge on human habitation looking for easy meals of garbage, throw-aways and highway road kills. They have been seen frolicking about in winter blizzards that no human could possibly endure, and, in fact, seem to be able to adapt to almost any condition or situation.

There have been other observations and research conducted on ravens, one by an American university. The basic premise was to put a tame raven (one held in captivity) on a perch and suspend a chunk of meat below the perch by a string, to see how long it would take for the raven to retrieve it (if at all). The basis of this experiment was to compare it to a crow. Let us first put this into perspective, to give you, the reader, an idea of how biased humans can be. This experiment could be compared to asking a human to stand on a round log, say about eight inches in diameter, with both hands tied behind their back and asking the human to do the same thing (get a piece of meat suspended below the log). I am including this comparative mental image to illustrate how humans bias everything we do because of our physical abilities. The situation was set up and controlled by humans who, without knowing, forced a raven to perform a task that humans consider to be a very simple test of intelligence. Sitting (or standing) on a log, a human could simply reach down and pull up the string with our hands, and retrieve the meat. The raven was placed in a situation made unfair by its physical limitations.

To give you an idea of how intelligent a raven is, it accomplished the feat in a few hours, by pulling the string up with its bill and then standing on the string to keep it from falling back. The crow failed to accomplish the task after many days of trying. What about the human? Could a human have retrieved the meat standing on the log with both hands tied behind their back to make it fair? The raven obviously does not possess hands. Well my guess is no unless you perhaps employed a skilled circus performer. The raven did it in a few hours. The raven overcame human bias to accomplish the task. Could a human do the same in a raven's environment? In fact, I think that the raven knew immediately what the situation was; all it had to do was figure out a way to overcome its physical limitations, and that involves logic and deductive reasoning.

Like most creatures, ravens have their own language to communicate with one another. They can and do easily imitate other birds, and do it sometimes just for fun. Next to humans, ravens are perhaps the most widely distributed and successful creatures on the planet. Researchers are just now beginning to realize how ravens have done this. They appear to have an exploitive nature and teach their young that human habitation means meals with minimal effort. Some researchers are currently pondering this exploitive ability that ravens possess, and are wondering how it came to exist. Well, my answer is, *they learned it from watching us.* So, who is exploiting whom?

Even common everyday, largely unnoticed, songbirds show some type of intelligence. The robin is one of the most intelligent of this group. Every year Canadians go out and rake their lawns, usually in the spring and fall. After every small section has had a garden rake passed over it to disturb debris and scarify the ground, a robin appears, usually within 10 to 15 minutes. It lands only on the area that has been raked, and proceeds to make an easy meal of disturbed grubs. Given that Canadian homeowners have been doing this only for a relatively short period of time (perhaps a few decades) this is an amazing ability. This is learned behavior on the part of the robin. Humans did not teach the robin to look for grubs and worms on a raked patch of grass; it somehow knew or reasoned and then remembered this. It is difficult to say whether each robin learns this individually or if the young are taught this trick. It is the only bird that I know of that does this.

Robins are very patient, efficient food collectors. While other birds, like starlings, strut about the lawn in a very aggressive manner, poking their heads down in the grass every foot or so and usually coming up empty, the robin patiently observes the scene, hopping two to four feet then stopping. It waits and looks, hops another few feet, then stops again. Within a very short time it displays amazingly keen sensory perception, hops over to a specific area, picks up the worm, and continues. Many other birds and creatures display amazing abilities, but humans are so lacking in awareness that they fail to see what is happening around them.

For many years humans have kept other mammals in captivity to study them (and entertain us), yet have failed to understand why mammals in captivity have such a low birth rate, while reproducing normally in the wild. *Perhaps they do not want to.* Perhaps they possess the ability to suppress their reproductive system because they do not want to bring any offspring into that kind of environment. It is also possible that human females once possessed the same ability, but have lost this capability because of thousands of years of aggression and because of lifestyle change, and increase in physical and emotional stress.

Modern day primates still fascinate humans. We continue to do our research and observations, primarily because we now know that they are related to us. Most researchers continue to concentrate on primates and ignore most of the other animals, including some who show more intelligence. One of the problems, of course, is that some of the most intelligent creatures are aquatic, which makes them rather difficult to interact with. That does not seem to have stopped humans from obsessively preoccupying themselves with the shark, which is one of the least intelligent creatures on the planet. The shark is one of the most primitive species, a remnant of the dinosaur age that is nothing more than an eating machine. That is not to say that studying sharks will not yield some benefit, but most of the human fascination seems to be primarily preoccupied with the sharks raw bestiality and the "danger" factor that it poses. There may be something in common here, as the Moderns seem to relate better to an aggressive, unintelligent killer than to gentler, more intelligent creatures.

Most of our data collection and observations on everything except primates is done almost solely for the purposes of trying to understand their instinctive behavior, yet we still refuse to accept that many of these creatures are just as advanced as we are, but in different ways. The fact that they would not pass a human intelligence test leads us to assume, rather ignorantly and arrogantly, that we are the supreme intelligence on this planet. What people fail to realize is that humans and primates are only one of many species of creatures that evolved over millions of years, and that it is impossible for highly evolved creatures not to have intelligence because that is how evolution works. It is impossible for every species of mammals (other than humans) to simply reach a definitive point and then stay there, or run entirely on instinct. They have as much intelligence as we do, and we just do not see it because of our limitations, our inability to look past the physical differences, because, generally, Moderns see only the most obvious.

Recently I watched a program on television—which could be a wonderful device for educational purposes—about some researchers studying sperm whales. When one of the whales came near, the researchers noticed that it could make whale-sound even while out of the water...how fascinating. However, that is not quite what I observed. A female sperm whale raised its head out of the water right beside the boat, looked directly at the humans floating on the surface, and made a deliberate attempt to communicate with the humans. When she did not receive an intelligent response, the whales went on their way.

The octopus, the dreaded monster of the deep, is also one of the most intelligent creatures on the planet. For years divers and researchers have observed the octopus in its natural environment and have wondered if it could think and reason because of some unusual occurrences. Even Jacques Cousteau and his team have researched the octopus and published books and material about it (See References), yet everyone stops short of actually saying that this unusual creature can do what only humans were thought to be able to do. When placed in situations that require conscious thought, the octopus can use reasoning to understand what is happening around it.

Interestingly, three of the most intelligent creatures on the planet—the whale, the dolphin, and the octopus—are ocean-dwellers, which is where life began millions of years ago. Perhaps scientists are looking in the wrong place to try to understand evolution. We continue to look in the one area that we have a very difficult time seeing, and all that does is foster our imagination of aliens. There is absolutely no question that creatures like the whale and dolphin are as intelligent as we are, and the fact that they, and many others, do not exploit other creatures for their survival other than for food may, in fact, make them more advanced socially than humans.

Much of the interpretation of the data collected on many of these creatures is based on humans being far more intelligent and all of this data has to be processed through human brains, which is the main reason that we arrogantly go on our way thinking that every other creature is inferior to us. One of the main reasons that we know so little about these creatures is humans cannot accept the possibility that creatures like whales, dolphins, and even the octopus are not only as intelligent as we are, but may in fact be more intelligent. Perhaps they are just waiting for us to catch up. It is not until humans accept this fact, that life on this planet will be completely understood. So, as we continue to dump toxic waste, garbage, raw sewage, and nuclear waste into the oceans, and use them like toilets, we are perhaps killing the only creatures that can give us the answers. Life began in the oceans; will it end there first? Will life on land follow?

There are perhaps some people, who think that we can just keep a few ocean creatures in captivity and study them there, but it does not work that way; I think that is pretty obvious now to most people.

As these creatures continue to congregate in areas like the west coast of Canada, where they feel safe, they are coming into conflict with one another. This is primarily due to many decades of whaling and poor fishing practices which have unbalanced the oceanic environment. So, not only have we totally disrupted the land-based ecology, but the aquatic one as well. Over the course of thousands of years, the Moderns have run roughshod over the planet, destroying everything in their path. Pretty intelligent! In the process of human evolution we have displaced many creatures from their natural habitat and greatly decimated others by our destructive behavior, while still others have hung on and managed to adapt and survive. The biggest problem is, of course, that humans do not have a *natural habitat*. Every other creature's *habitat is our habitat*; they have had to learn to cope with us. It is they who have learned to live with humans, but have humans learned to live with them?

These other creatures have influenced every aspect of our society, yet we continue to exploit and kill them with very little concern. We incorporate some characteristic of some other mammal, bird or other creature in just about everything we do. We want to be as strong as a bull, as powerful as a lion, as fast and graceful as a gazelle, as agile as a cat, to soar like an eagle, or swim like a dolphin. We build machines, such as automobiles, to emulate some of the above, and many people are drawn to a particular car because of its sleek design and exotic name. Why is it that we want so badly to be like them? If we are superior to them, why do we consistently copy them? Many of our achievements were the direct result of studying nature. The main reason we do this is to make up for our inadequacies. We built the airplane to fly. We have sonar and radar similar to a dolphin and a bat, and the list is lengthy. We build powerful machines to make up for our physical weakness. We need everything we build to *replace* our lost natural instincts and abilities—not because we are superior or more intelligent. Our physical abilities and our limitless habitat requirements allow us to move freely and observe and mimic all of the other creatures.

Humans invented weapons because they needed to kill, something our ancestors never needed to do. They just hung out in the trees and ate fruit all day. Weapons were the human equivalent to the natural weapons the other carnivores had, such as claws, teeth, and powerful limbs and jaws. Humans need guns because they're *afraid.*

The truth is that the human race is an *anomaly, a deviation from the natural order*. We are the only species to start out as something different than we are now. We are the only species that does not know where we belong. All of the other creatures know what they are and where they belong and fit in. We do not.

If humans had the intelligence to do so, every creature on the planet could be ranked in order of intelligence. Everything from the most highly evolved mammal to the smallest, simplest creatures has some form of intelligence. What is intelligence anyway? Humans seem to think that they have plenty, yet they do not know what it is or how to define it. Is intelligence having a high degree of awareness? If so humans would fail because even a crow has better awareness than most humans. Is intelligence the ability to build a car? Only humans need cars; dolphins can swim where they want to go, and ravens can fly. They do not need cars. Is intelligence the ability to play classical music? If you allowed a chimpanzee to play with a simple musical instrument and that knowledge was passed down for hundreds of years to successive generations, eventually even a chimp could probably play classical music, much as humans have done (maybe not as well). A chimp doesn't care if it plays classical music, only humans do. Is intelligence a learned ability or a natural ability? For humans it is entirely a learned ability, which does not necessarily make humans better. Would an intelligent creature destroy its own habitat and threaten its own extinction?

If you could take a young human between two and four years old who had only the ability to find enough food to survive and put him or her out in the middle of nowhere, naked, and leave him or her there for about 25 years, what do you suppose you'd find? Chances are that after 25 years you'd find a 27- to 29-year-old human, naked, with just enough intelligence to find food to survive. Without another human to show them what to do, or to copy, humans are entirely helpless right from birth. So, to a human, what is learned (or taught) is all important.

When humans are born, they are entirely helpless and even have to be shown how to feed to survive. For most humans intelligence is based on whatever education or "input" they have into their brain throughout life, but most importantly while growing up. That is why I have chosen the term *condition* when referring to the process humans use to learn. It is not so much *learning* as it is *conditioning*. Without any natural instinct to rely on for help, we are only as good as our evolution or progression allows us to be. Throughout our evolution, humans have very slowly accumulated knowledge that we continue to add to over time. We are not born intelligent; we just have the potential to have intelligence. How each individual absorbs whatever knowledge they accumulate will affect what that individual knows and does for life.

Ignorance is the biggest threat to the human race.

* * *

Ignorance breeds fear which ultimately breeds prejudice and aggression.

Perhaps the only chance humans have now is to have an educational system that places the environment first and everything else comes second. Since humans are conditioned as they grow to adulthood, perhaps conditioning them to believe that the environment is the most important aspect of life is their only hope for the future.

Because we force-feed limited knowledge as humans grow to adulthood, this essentially is conditioning. Learning is something entirely different. To *learn* is more of a voluntary act, and far more humans would continue to learn throughout their lives if we only knew how. Most humans stop the knowledge input process as soon as they leave school, and from then on it is primarily just trial and error, or learning from experience.

So the key is to want to learn throughout life. Instead of conditioning little humans to be exploiters and consumers, perhaps we should be conditioning them to be able to interact with their environment, instead of being afraid of it.

So, are humans the most intelligent? Based on 30+ years of observation, my opinion is probably no. Either the sperm whale or the orca (killer whale) is probably the most intelligent creature on the planet. Is the average human as intelligent as the average raven? Probably! Will humans ever be the most intelligent creatures on the planet? Maybe, one day!

Humans have a very large brain compared to their body size, but how much we use our brain is still under debate. The most common theory is still about 10%, so what is the other 90% doing, and can it be utilized? If humans have such a large brain and rely on learning to function, why do we stop after we reach adulthood? Many readers are disagreeing right now because they think that they continue to learn throughout life. Is stumbling along by trial and error the same as learning and consciously stimulating the brain with a constant flow of relevant information? It appears as though humans have yet to figure out how to access the entire brain, and what information to feed it when they do in order to promote more, or more constant brain stimulation. Humans require constant brain stimulation throughout life;

otherwise any previously learned knowledge is slowly lost. It is only through the constant stimulation of the brain with relevant information, and retaining it throughout life, so that knowledge is accumulative, that humans may eventually understand and be, perhaps, the most intelligent creature on the planet.

The big questions are, when will that happen and will the other highly evolved creatures survive to that point? I do not know. Humans are in quite a quandary as they are abnormal to the natural order of evolution that got us here, and may not be the most intelligent creature on the planet.

If you will remember back a few chapters, humans got this far primarily because of their hands (physical abilities), and not because of intelligence. Have humans evolved to adapt and out compete (and eliminate) the other highly evolved creatures? Do we, or should we, make a conscious decision to stop exploiting and killing them? Can we make a conscious decision to live with them without destroying habitats and exploiting them? Do the majority of humans even care? What would life be like without them? How many humans would even notice? What will life be like if we continue on the current path? The fact is all of these decisions will probably be made for us, because we do not, at this point, have the ability to make them for ourselves.

THE FINAL CHAPTER

Everything changed the day we walked out of the forest, about five million or so years ago. We started to lose the natural instincts that applied to forest life and had evolved with us over many years. We did not have time to develop new ones, so we did whatever we had to do to survive. We exploited whatever resources were at hand, and five millions years later, well… you know the story. We are just now beginning to see the results of that exploitation.

The current world economy, and in fact our entire existence, is based on exploiting the environment. We now know that the environment is being threatened, so if we save the environment, which we must do to survive, on what will we base our economies? As we start the next millennium, the human race is approaching a crossroads, another major fork in our evolutionary path. Interestingly, it may be evolution that provides the answers. As mentioned previously, the world is currently in an economic dilemma (stagnant, bordering recession) and it will be our economic situation that takes us into the future.

Most are aware of the term *globalization,* which is circulating in social circles and conversations everywhere. However, very few people seem to understand exactly what the term means. Some commonly refer to it as a kind of coming together or somehow being more in touch with other parts of the world via the Internet and other technologies, or business and economics converging on a global level. All of these are essentially correct, but something else is also happening. Globalization is not so much a collapse of the global economy as it is a shrinkage and decline. Once the process has worked its way through, *society will take a different direction.* Many people will find themselves having to be more self-reliant and depending less on government and society to provide for them. For some people this will not be a huge problem, however, for many dependents, it might be.

In the last half of the twentieth century we managed to evolve far enough to understand the very basics of life. Genetic study has led the human race to the ability to alter the very genetic makeup of a biological organism. This was the narrow path that scientists took because of Wallace's (and Darwin's) work. If we can alter it, does that mean that we fully understand it? Over the last 10,000 years humans have, unknowingly, done a great deal of damage, not only to the environment, but also to ourselves. So are we genetically altering food (and potentially humans) to somehow make up for, or correct these mistakes? Could these mistakes correct themselves if left alone? Currently scientists are developing genetically manipulated domestic animals, their hope being that they can spawn new animals that have internal organs that will not be rejected if transplanted into humans, as well as cure many diseases and disorders.

Will they then directly transplant animal genes into humans? Will there be a demand for hawk genes to improve eyesight or lion genes to improve strength? Will humans become a "cross-section" of other animals? You know the ones—the animals that we consider to be inferior and continue to destroy on a daily basis.

In our dependent society, many have come to rely on scientists and other specialists to lead us into the future. The only problem is that, generally speaking, scientists maintain the attitude that, we are the supreme intelligence and if we can do it in the laboratory, then it is a major step forward in our progression and is... OK; but is it? Let me just nudge your memory with *nuclear technology*. The plants that produce our nuclear energy are proving to be far too expensive to maintain and run, and we, as yet, do not know how to rid ourselves of the deadly wastes produced by them.

In this century we have also managed to recombine naturally occurring chemicals (as well as man made) to produce substances that are used primarily to kill naturally occurring biological organisms, including ourselves. Many of these recombined chemicals were developed to control or eliminate some of the smallest, lesser-evolved creatures, such as viruses, bacteria, and insects, to make our lives "better" (and to make money). Does the fact that all we have managed to do is make them stronger suggest that we have failed and should reassess this practice, or should we step-up the war on these little creatures? Who is outsmarting whom? I think we are all familiar with the term *biological warfare*. Sometimes it applies to us.

Quite recently a white scientist from South Africa admitted publically that the white Afrikaner government was actively involved in biological warfare development. They were experimenting with a wide variety of viruses and bacteria to see if they could 'create' a weapon that would specifically target black Africans. Their objective was to secretly kill black people (CBS: 60 minutes). One of the viruses that they were experimenting with was a monkey virus. AIDS is caused by a monkey virus. Coincidence? I doubt that we will ever know for sure. Society could never accept such a revelation as it could be comparable to something like the holocaust of Nazi Germany surely something like that could never happen again.

These human-made unnatural substances are now proving that humans have physical abilities that exceed our combined intellectual capabilities, and many of these substances will persist in the natural environment for years. We have no idea what effect they may have. Until the last half of the twentieth century, the earth relied on evolution to guide the development of all biological organisms. Has evolution done a pretty fair job, or should humans take over that role?

Once this path is chosen and enough changes occur, then the path is set, and there is no reversing it.

The fact that we have tried to control many other creatures with our "supreme intelligence", however small they are, but could not, should provide a valuable indication of our abilities at this point. There are some inherent problems with this aspect of our society. If a person spends too much time in the world of academia, working on ideas, either original or existing, then the tendency is to lose touch with the rest of the world, because of this narrowly-focused endeavor. At the same time there are many people who are proficient when dealing with life on a more general level, but remain very narrow-minded. Each may succeed (at least in theory) in their respective area, but not in both, and therefore receives limited benefit. This is the characteristic of a society where each segment relies on another segment in order to function, and so no one ever understands the whole equation.

If the global economy continued to shrink, much of the financial resources that researchers rely on to continue their work, would no longer be available. Work being done in areas like genetically altered foods, cloning, and chemical research, not to mention further exploitation of the environment, may be very limited. Perhaps this would be a good time to reassess the situation and ponder which areas are actually beneficial and which are potentially dangerous.

As the global economy shrinks, communities here in Canada will continue to amalgamate and governments will continue to download responsibility to a more local level. This transition will cause many concerns because it involves change. Businesses will also continue to amalgamate and many communities will find companies and industries pulling out of their communities leaving residents to wonder where they will acquire such basic necessities as food. Communities will need to become more self-sufficient and many will start forming co-operatives. These co-operatives may rely on local farms to supply much of their food. In the not-too-distant future water and land (primarily farmland) will be the most valuable resources. As banks close branches, people will form their own credit unions to see to their local economies, and so on.

As social programs and employment opportunities shrink, there will be a move to change the local economies and people will exchange services as opposed to selling them.

As the economy and the tax base shrink, social programs that we now take for granted will be severely cut to the point where communities will have to provide for themselves. Many facets of our society, such as policing, basic health care, and education, will be the sole responsibility of each community. Programs are based on tax dollars and so as the tax base shrinks, the social programs will be reduced; as programs are reduced people will assume (rightly so) that they should pay less tax. Eventually, the society that we know now will no longer exist in the not-to-distant future.

The Western democracies are on the brink of facing Third World conditions as there will be shortages and disruptions in the supply of food and water, as well as a rise in disease and sickness. Only then will people rethink the situation.

All of these changes will allow people to have more say in how society is to be structured and which direction it will go. It is important for people to understand that these changes are not the end of the world, and some changes may, at first, appear as though we are going backwards. Some will be positive and some, perhaps, negative, and many may say "history is repeating itself again". Not really, evolution is just painfully slow at times.

Throughout history the most aggressive, least self-reliant humans have controlled society simply because of their position of power and wealth. Until now the masses were, for the most part, uneducated, naive and largely ignored, but that has changed and the world will change because of it.

Perhaps as we go into this millennium, we can all come back to Earth and get our house in order here, before we go looking in space for other forms of life that we do not understand.

Why are Moderns so intent on going into space? Why do they want so badly to get off the planet? Is it because they do not understand it? Is it because they know they are destroying it? Let us find somewhere else to live, because this landfill (Earth) is going to be full soon. Scientists insist that they can find other life forms in the universe and world leaders perhaps need somewhere else to go just in case things get out of hand. Are Moderns somehow hoping that a more intelligent life form will come along and save us from ourselves? What alien in its right mind would want to have anything to do with such an aggressive, primitive species as humans?

As human evolution goes, we are still in our infancy; we have evolved just far enough to become aware of our place in this incredibly vast universe, but not yet to the point of finding out if we are really alone. We may never know.

All of the answers can be found here on this planet. All we have to do is look for them.

Currently the goal is to explore Mars but the Moderns are going to find Mars just a little beyond their reach. It took a tremendous amount of resources to land on the moon; just getting to the next planet will prove to be insurmountable.

* * *

So have we reached the peak? Is our empire built? Are we just maintaining it now? What exactly are we working for? Are we, in fact, in decline much like the Roman Empire and every other society developed by the Moderns?

Well, it looks that way and, as we decline, an interesting social shift is taking place. For at least the last 3,500 years, modern men have developed and randomly steered which direction civilization would go. Most recently the global economy, society, and in fact the entire planet has been controlled or influenced primarily by white men or Europeans and their descendants. As we start the next millennium women and all others (aboriginals and other races of people) have been gaining ground and are quickly establishing a foothold in many societies. They are fast becoming, if not equals, then at the very least, a major influence.

Most people see this as a major advancement in our modern societies, and it is, but not for the reasons they think. This social shift is not because modern men are suddenly becoming more socially aware; it is because men are losing their grip on society. As we decline there are far more women and races of people who are better educated than in the past. Historically the males controlled society and were careful to maintain control. They are now losing that control. As we progress into the millennium there will be a tendency for society controlled primarily by dependent modern males to continue to oppress any change primarily because the modern males are accustomed to having others do for them. To translate into a more practical and perhaps more visible social dynamic, there will be a move toward the "Big Brother" scenario. This aspect of society has intrigued many people for years, but most don't realize that it has been in our society since the beginning of civilization.

It is when societies decline that it becomes more noticeable, because modern society has always been based on controlling and exploiting the common masses. When the society stumbles, the wealthy elite and governments simply tighten the rein. As we decline, the current society is developing, and will continue to develop, a more rigid, intolerant mentality which may persist for many generations. It's all about whom controls whom. If we are in a decline will others take advantage of our situation here in Canada just as Moderns have done throughout history? Quite likely. Who will that be? Probably the United States and Britain as they have always wanted what we have; their presence will be more visible as time goes on. Canadians can expect to see more and more people with American and British accents appearing out of nowhere, intent on "showing us the way", even though we have done quite nicely without them until now.

Are we now positioned to go into a period of chaos and confusion that has inevitably followed after societies hit their peak? Are we prepared for another Dark Age? We will see.

So it may be the rapid shrinkage of the economy which may allow people to pick which path we should take. Many people will choose a more *natural path* into the future, but what percentage of society will that be? Have there already been enough changes in the recent past to alter the evolutionary path that got us here? Should we allow evolution to help us out, or should we continue to assume that we can do it ourselves? Are we patting ourselves on the back into extinction? Our track record is not that great.

Over the last 1500 years the Germanics (Europeans) have considered themselves to be the center of science, medicine, and all of the discoveries that went along with them. The Germanics followed up any advancement that the Greeks, Romans, or Egyptians had made, but they could not have achieved the present technology by themselves. It took the multicultural societies and their ethnic mix of people and ideas to get us to where we are now, but because Europeans and their descendants insisted on controlling the entire world and everyone on it, we all had to follow their path whether we wanted to or not. That path leads us to teetering on the brink of destruction. Primarily left-brain European mathematical thinking along with the business capabilities of the Jewish peoples has taken this society as far as it can.

Given their historical inability to understand the Ancients, it appears that Moderns and the Germanics in particular, have limited access to the brain's right hemisphere. Through several decades of brain research, scientists have discovered that the left and right sides of the brain can actually function independently if the primary link, the corpus callosum, is severed. The left hemisphere is considered to be somewhat fragmented and primarily deals with mathematics, language, logic, and reasoning, while the right side has better perceptual and spatial awareness and grasps things as a whole.

Interestingly, most researchers in these areas have historically been people of Germanic descent.

How Westerners can consider themselves superior when the vast majority know absolutely nothing (or very little) about other peoples and their cultures is a mystery.

Over the last several centuries civilization has been preoccupied with advancing science, medicine, and building what has become the global economy. The people of civilization view all of this as evolving and progressing. Many people see our physical accomplishments and are lead to believe that we are in control of this planet and are evolving toward... something.

Moderns live in a society that feels the need to move forward toward something but at the same time, are apprehensive and fear change. Most people today call the Western democracies "modern", but most are far from being truly modern. Canada made some advancement in social reform prior to civilization reaching its peak in the 1970s, and could possibly be considered modern. Unlike the U.S., most of our resources went into social development as opposed to arms, and Canada, overall, perhaps has the best social programs of all Modern countries. That is not to say we are perfect. Canada is a classic example of a democracy, in that it has a majority consisting of one type of people, in this case white Christians. We allow immigrants to settle here and "contribute" to our society, but are very careful to always maintain the white majority to ensure dominance.

This has been the stereotypical democracy since classic Greece.

The United States is similar in make-up, but because the U.S. made very little progress in the way of social reforms, it continues to live in the year 1776. Their reluctance to update the original constitution has allowed the society to disintegrate from the inside as crime, homelessness, and polarity between rich and poor have only been exacerbated. People create a society and the society reflects the people.

I am not sure what year Europe is living in.

Neither Canada nor the United States has atoned for the atrocities inflicted on the native peoples of North America. We did our best to either eradicate or assimilate them but they managed to hold on and it may be they who can help lead us into the future. Most Moderns believe that the Ancient cultures were backward thinking, because they believed that life continued in a cycle. The Ancients believed that life was created from the earth, water, or sky and each creature fulfilled a destiny or role; when their time had come they either returned from where they originated, or some were thought to pass into a world beyond or a netherworld, thus completing the cycle. This cyclic belief allowed the ancient cultures to live in balance with their environment, and gave them a better understanding of the other creatures that they co-existed with.

Moderns still cringe when mention is made about the sacrifices that the ancient cultures performed, and there is no argument that it did happen. Moderns find this very distasteful and barbaric. Yet every year on November 11th the Moderns of Western democracies take time out to pay their respects to millions of war dead who were sacrificed. Is it the same? I will let you decide. Essentially what is happening is that the modern dependent, or least self-reliant people of the world require all of these facets of their society (science, medicine, and so on) in order to eventually understand themselves and life on the planet Earth. Over the last 2000 or so years they have been, unknowingly, working toward that goal.

Only when the Moderns, or people of "civilization", come to the end of their evolutionary path, and reach that goal, and *understand*, can descendants of the Ancients and the other mammals and creatures and the rest of nature carry on where they left off, before they were so viciously disrupted and exploited.

Most Moderns mistakenly believe that they are supremely intelligent because they can say they are intelligent. Moderns 50 years ago thought the same thing, and Moderns 200 years ago also thought the same thing, and Moderns 500 years ago and 2000 years ago also thought the same thing. We are actually still quite barbaric; we just do not realize it, because we have nothing to compare ourselves to. Apparently we've gone from not realizing that we could, in fact, think for ourselves, to being highly intelligent in about 300 years. That's pretty remarkable.

At some point in the future, the people of civilization *will understand life and its meaning*, and what they will discover is essentially what most of the Ancients had discovered thousands of years ago; there is no meaning *of* life; or *to* life; there just *is* life.

The reason humans dominate the planet is simply because we are the *most aggressive* and not because we are the *most intelligent*. The planet will always be here, the question is, what will live on it? As we proceed into the future and the European-based society declines, many of the Ancients will now be able to go their own way. The Moderns can either come along or get lost in their own anarchy. Perhaps when we re-emerge on the other side (chaos/dark age) we may live in a truly civilized society for the first time in our history.

I am only one member of the human race and one of the creatures who enjoys this planet, and greatly respects the ancient cultures and what they had achieved; as much as it pains me to say this, everything that has happened to this point, had to happen, because that is how evolution works. So, our future is still in the hands of the evolutionary gods. Despite the fact that my ancestors, the Celts, may have been the first people in recorded history to be persecuted and ethnically "cleansed" (by Julius Caesar) and that humans are poised to kill many of the most intelligent creatures on the planet, it is hard to place blame because two thousand years ago, a very wise human said, "forgive them, for they know not what they do". He was absolutely right, and that statement still holds true.

REFERENCES

Aldebert et al, *Illustrated History of Europe,* Weidenfeld and Nicolson, 1992.

Asimov, Isaac, Eyes on the Universe, 1975.

Brantl, G., editor, *Catholicism,* George Braziller, Inc., 1962.

Chalmers, David M., Hooded Americanism: History of the Ku Klux Klan, 1865 to 1965, Doubleday and Company, Inc., 1965.

Cousteau, Jacques-Ives, and Philippe Diole, *Octopus and Squid: The Soft Intelligence,* A. & W Publishers, c.1975.

Darwin, Charles, *The Origin of Species,* first published 1859.

Dunstan, J. L., editor, *Protestantism,* George Braziller, Inc., 1962.

Durant, Will, *Caesar and Christ,* Simon and Schuster, 1944.

Fincher, Jack, The Human Body: The Brain, Mystery of Matter and Mind, Torstar Books Inc., 1984.

Gibbons, E[Edward], *The Decline and Fall of the Roman Empire,* Rand McNally and Company, 1974.

Hanson, Victor D., *The Wars of the Ancient Greeks,* Cassell, 1999.

Haywood, John, The Illustrated History of Early Man, Bison Books, 1995.

Herm, Gerhard, The Celts: The People Who Came of out the Darkness, St. Martin's Press, 1975.

Hertzberg, A., editor, *Judaism,* George Braziller, Inc., 1962.

Hertzberg, A., editor, *Islam*, George Braziller, Inc, 1962.

James, Simon, *The World of the Celts*, Thames and Hudson, 1993.

Moffat, Alistair, *Arthur and the Lost Kingdoms*, Weidenfeld and Nicolson, 1999.

Morris, Desmond, *The Naked Ape*, Jonathan Cape, 1967.

Oliver, Martyn, History of Philosophy: Great Thinkers from 600 BC to the Present Day, Prospero Books, 1999.

Paris, Erna, *The End of Days*, Lester Publishing, 1995.

Restak, Richard, M.D., *The Brain*, Bantam Books, 1984.

Sagan, Carl, *Cosmos*, Random House, 1980.

Springer, Sally, and George Deutsch, *Left Brain, Right Brain*, W.H. Freeman and Company, 1981.

Stearns, Peter M., Impact of the Industrial Revolution, Protest, and Alienation, Prentice Hall, 1972.

Sulloway, Frank J., *Born to Rebel*, Random House, 1996.

Tisdall, Paul, *In Search of Human Origins*, Canadian Broadcasting Corporation, 1981.

Wendt, Herbert, From Ape to Adam: the search for the ancestry of man, Thames and Hudson, 1972.

Weyer, Edward, Jr., *Primitive Peoples Today*, Doubleday and Company Inc., c.1959.

Wright, Ronald, Time Among the Maya: Travels in Belize, Guatemala, and Mexico, Viking, 1989.

The Times Atlas of World History, Hammond, fourth edition, 1994.

Made in the USA
Lexington, KY
20 November 2019